# Being the LEADER

## A Guide to Leadership in Network Marketing

Ryan Daley

Dedicated to-
*Every person who has ever believed they could make a positive impact through Network Marketing.*

# TABLE OF CONTENTS

Acknowledgments     i

Introduction     1

     *Why the Book Came to Be*     3

     *How to Get the Most Out of This Book*     7

1   Being the Leader     11

     *A Leader*     13

     *Personal Responsibility*     15

     *Self-Eliminating Leadership*     17

     *Leader of One*     19

     *You Are a Creator*     21

     *Realize the Potential in Others*     23

2   Development of One     25

     *The Importance of Developing Oneself*     27

     *Personal Development*     29

     *The Forever Student*     31

     *Finding the Time*     33

     *Remain Teachable*     37

*Seek to Be, Rather than to Find*     39

*Your Environment*     41

*Habits*     45

*Money Magnifies*     49

3   Leadership Building Philosophies     51

*Introducing Leadership Building Philosophies*     53

*Like Attracts Like*     55

*The Pipeline*     57

*The Harvest and The Planting*     59

*Finding the Three (or the Three Hundred)*     61

*Understanding Momentum*     63

*Applying, Teaching, and Training on Momentum*     65

*JUST GO, APPLY, AND DO IT!*     67

*Repetition*     69

*Common Denominator*     71

4   Leadership Perspective     73

*Managing Your Perspective – True Key to Success*     75

*The Cut of Leadership*     77

*Defined by Your Success NOT Your Failure*     81

*Manage Your "Arrival" and "Why is My Business Stalled?"*     83

*Never Judge Others' Potential*     87

*Managing Personal-Professional Relationships*     91

*What You Do or Don't Do*     95

*Being the Top 5% - Easier Than You Think*     99

*Pace Someone Faster (Marathon Part 1)*     101

*Consistency (Marathon Part 2)*     103

*Avoid Boredom (Marathon Part 3)*     105

*Know When to Look Up and When to Look Down (Marathon Part 4)*     109

*No Excuses*     111

*Are You Serving?*     113

5   Leadership Duplication     115

*Duplication*     117

*Maximizing Two Different Duplications*     119

*Master Your Message*        123

*Repetition Is the Law of Learning*        125

*The Last Temptation of the Pleaser*        127

*Share, Share, Share*        129

6    Leadership Finances        131

*Finances of a Leader*        133

*Retail Sales – The Foundation for Stability*        137

*"The Tax Man" Account – 30%*        139

*A Generous Giver is a Generous Receiver – 10%*        141

*Pay Your Most Important Employee – 10%*        145

*Pay Your Most Important Supporters – 10%*        147

*Reinvest in Your Business – 10%*        149

*Removing Your Nightmares and Fulfilling Your Dreams – 30%*        151

# BEING THE LEADER

# ACKNOWLEDGMENTS

In an industry where the entire concept of success is found in making connections, and allowing yourself to influence and be influenced by others, there are too many people that have impacted the content of this book, both directly and indirectly, to acknowledge here. To those people unmentioned, know that I love you, I appreciate you, and I will never forget you. I would like to thank directly Haylie Hoglund, a dear friend who has probably trusted me more than she should have throughout our careers together. Her willingness to review, edit, and give honest, transparent, and sometimes hurtful feedback is more appreciated than she will know.

# Introduction

RYAN DALEY

## Why This Book Came to Be

After my first decade of working in the Network Marketing Industry with the best that the industry had to offer, I took for granted the concepts of leadership as common knowledge - particularly the basics. I had helped some of the largest leaders in the industry grow larger, move their teams, find new companies, and develop training programs for their organizations. I had worked with numerous companies on leadership recruitment and development strategies, compensation and incentive plans, and a slew of other projects.

I had reached a place where I was surrounded by a culture of leadership, that had somewhat lost sight of the basic principles of leadership along the way.

It was at this moment in my life that I had what some might call a mid-career crisis. Frustration, resentment, and countless other negative emotions flooded in as a result of external forces in the industry – and I stumbled upon something remarkable. I found a small start-up company with something that I believed was truly different. My suspicions were confirmed and I realized I had found exactly what I needed to feel good about Network Marketing again.

Soon I found myself removed from my established, stable leadership environment – as my commitment to this new project required me to relocate. It was a fresh start, with a fresh company, and with a fresh idea. We were on a roll, and the growth was remarkable! The strategy that we had developed had truly given an opportunity to everyone to find success, which meant that generally speaking, everyone who wanted success got it!

This presented me with an entirely new business struggle that I never imagined having before – the need to develop leadership. Keep in mind, this was not the development of the seeds of leadership that were planted – but the development of leadership where no leadership existed before. The entire organization was built

3

by stay-at-home moms who had never been in a leadership role before in their lives; whether at school, church, or even in their families (in some circumstances). And here they were with success, many of them being thrust into leadership roles they never would have fathomed they could have achieved before.

I had heard (and seen) companies outgrowing their manufacturing and distribution processes, and even their cash flow; but I had never heard of a company outgrowing their leadership. Having focused on developing leaders before, I jumped in and started to work with these newly appointed leaders, I quickly realized how much I had taken for granted! Even the basic concepts that I had been surrounded with previously were received as brand new ideas. It quickly became evident that there was a foundation of basic leadership knowledge that was missing. I had never seen these concepts covered, nor addressed in other leadership programs. Many of these programs had also taken for granted some of these basic concepts – which might have explained the low adoption rates; even the leaders in the industry suffered from perception bias, being unable themselves to see the basic principles that helped them reach success.

This required me to get back to the basics that had never really needed to be vocalized before. As a result, it created a greater understanding of the basic stepping stones through the foundation of leadership and right into the halls of great leadership. We were able to walk through these basic concepts with these new-born leaders, and build them up into industry giants. These basic concepts then became the foundation for anyone to adopt a leadership path that was simple to follow. It became the groundwork of partnering with the company that anyone could succeed with, and aided in developing leadership in anyone who was willing to put forth the effort to do so. It was a natural marriage that generated unprecedented results.

This book is designed to help anyone who is willing, to start from any level, evolve their leadership skills within themselves and their organizations. It includes everything from basic concepts and principles to more advanced strategies, taught in a way that allows anyone to apply and learn from them. It is a concentrated outline of everything that a leader needs to know at any level to find even greater success than what they see now.

# How to Get the Most Out of This Book

The construction of this book is based upon a number of parts, with a number of sections within each part. Although the book is intended to be read from cover to cover, it is not a "one sitting book." It should be nibbled on. Each section is short, by design, and will allow you to read something quickly and then take some time to absorb the concept.

In an effort to help you get the most out of the book, and to offer some advice on the process with which you should work through this information, let me make you a promise: Everything in this book applies – even if you currently do not believe it does.

I would first recommend that you read through the entire book from cover to cover. Get an idea of the general principles and concepts that are taught. As you do this, you will discover things that ring true to you right now. You will notice that many of the sections are describing things that you are seeing or have seen in your business – and they will immediately resonate with you as true. Mark those things! Then when you are finished, go and re-read those sections.

After re-reading them, and even while you are going through the first time, make a conscious plan to apply the principles or lessons in your business. Be specific in what actions you are going to take, or what you will be adding to your business to get the results you want from that principle, and then go and do it. You can read all of the books in the world on any principle you want, but if you don't apply the knowledge you've gained, you will have only wasted your time and money.

Now as you are reading through the book for first time, pay special attention to the sections that you don't believe apply to you. You will not need to re-read those the first time, but make sure that you understand those concepts even if they do not apply to you. The reason that I ask you to do that is because I know that they will apply eventually. The most common thing I have ever heard from the leaders I have helped develop in my career was, "When you taught me that principle, I didn't believe it applied to me, until later – and then I realized YOU WERE RIGHT!"

In this book I do not talk about things that apply to some and not to others – although I could probably fill another book with those things. I have only included concepts that apply to all people within Network Marketing. These are truths that have not only been tested and proven to be true, they are principles that, when acknowledged and applied, have changed lives.

So even when you come across sections that you do not agree with, or think that they do not apply – still try and learn the principle. I promise you that in your business there will be a day when you will say, "He was right!" And you will want to go back and find that section again.

With that in mind, the next thing that I would recommend you do is identify the leaders within your organization and get this book into their hands. A funny thing will happen as you read through the first time. While reading a section, someone on your team will come to mind and you will think, "That is exactly what they need to hear." Write names in the margins of people who come to mind in each section. Then go through the book and make sure that everyone that came to mind gets a copy. Do everything you can to empower the leaders in your team with the same knowledge. Even those sections that you don't think yet apply to you – might very well immediately apply to someone on your team. The quicker you learn the concepts, the faster you can be a great leader. The quicker your team can learn these concepts, the faster you can create a powerhouse organization.

The final thing I would recommend is to schedule time every year to re-read the book. Refresh yourself on the principles that apply, those that don't apply (so you think), and those that didn't apply but you have learned now do apply. No matter how good your memory is, everyone can use a refresher course. It is through these regular readings that you will recall how a concept really did work, and you can recommit to implement it into your business.

In conclusion, the way to get the most out of this book is to: read it, apply it, share it, and then read it again.

# Part 1
# Being the Leader

RYAN DALEY

# A Leader

Throughout life we have regularly heard cliché terms in relation to people in history being natural born leaders. It is as if we are saying that they were born with the ability to speak, inspire, and motivate others to action. When we say this, we neglect a number of realities that ultimately distort the perception of ourselves and our own potential.

In some aspects, being a leader (as a skill) is no more different than being a remarkable pianist or painter. There are those in the world who have been called natural artists, but there are many more that are applauded for their skills who may not fit into this category. The reality that should never be overlooked is that even the greatest "natural" artist was not born with this skill. They may have had certain temperaments and natural physical abilities that gave them an advantage (e.g. the large handed ten key spread that is often needed for some of the more difficult pieces of music, or healthy eyesight for picking color tones), but each of them have had to learn simple concepts first. They then practice and develop their skills for years with sweat, dedication, and sacrifice. I suspect that no "natural" talent would look so natural to us if we could witness the process of practice and training to hone that skill from the very beginning.

In addition to this, leadership is not a skill or trait that compares to those classified as "talents," as genuine leadership is not an extension or enhancement by physical properties. This means that leadership is even further away from something that people are born with. It is a characteristic of someone who has developed leadership within themselves. Consequently, whether you believe this or not, this means that leadership is something that anyone can develop, and that everyone has the potential to have.

Now before you question or doubt the reality of that statement, realize that leadership looks different in different people. This is because every person is different; with different wants, desires, and motivations. Each one reading this book (and every member of your team currently or in the future) has different skills, different dreams, and, most importantly, different experiences from life. These differences do not limit one's ability to have leadership, but changes what the leadership would look like in their lives.

Leadership in one's life is manifested in quiet confidence, where leadership in another person's life is seen as bold, fearless, and extraverted gestures. This is not evidence of different levels of leadership – just different manifestations of it. Leadership isn't seen in outward manifestations of the leader, as much as it is seen in the responses of those being led.

This is the joy of leadership, particularly in the Network Marketing Industry. Everyone can be a leader, because everyone can learn to be a leader. This acknowledgement is one of the most critical keystones to your success – not just believing and working towards your own leadership success, but realizing that every member of your team has the potential to be a leader as well. That is real success! That is where real freedom is found, and that is the complete goal: Duplication! Leadership duplication is the process of building a team of self-motivated leaders.

In Network Marketing, it is not enough for you to be a leader of one. You need to be a leader of many leaders: a Leader of Leaders. This will be discussed more later.

Throughout history, there have been millions of people – MILLIONS of people – who are normal people, who have developed leadership in their own way and have done remarkable things. These are normal people, with normal genetics, normal lives, a normal history, and normal abilities – but they have, in one form or fashion, done remarkable things with their leadership skills.

You are no different than they are. You have the potential to do more than you are doing now. You have the potential to be more than you are being now. You have it within your nature, as they did within theirs to be phenomenal. It takes effort and work, but the reward is worth it.

# Personal Responsibility

We live in a world where it has become more common for members of society to feel entitled. Children are raised and taught from a very young age that others will provide for them. Teenagers are rarely asked to work in order to contribute to the home (financially or through chores). College students are encouraged to incur debt, and then do everything they can to avoid paying it back. There are some aspects of these statements that are seen as progression within society, and indeed they can be signs of that. Unfortunately, as members of this generation mature, they are never taught the realities of personal responsibility.

Some of those reading this book may have been in that boat, and many may actually still be there. There is no shame in this being the case; unless you realize this is the case and do nothing about it.

The only path to success within Network Marketing and in developing leadership within yourself and your organization is the path of personal responsibility. Within this entitlement generation, it is easy to "sell" Network Marketing when you discuss the concept of leverage and the ability to make money from other people's work. Too often, this pitch is used to recruit the entitled generation, only to discover that they don't put any work into their own business – and therefore can never reap the rewards. This business is not about earning off of other's labors – it is about building others, helping others find success, and, in turn, be rewarded for that. Success in leadership and in Network Marketing is founded upon personal responsibility.

It doesn't matter what your company's compensation plan is. It doesn't matter what your product is, or what your company does in the marketplace. Your success is no one's responsibility but your own. Each leader has had to learn the motto, "If it is to be, it is up to me!"

There are times when people complain that it shouldn't be that way. "If I was only with this upline leader, or placed in that position, I would have the support I need to be successful." This attitude isn't leadership. This is weakness, coupled with excuses and petitions to justify laziness. No matter what anyone says when they signed you up, or how the compensation plan will do this or that, it ultimately will be based upon what you do that will define your success – not what anyone else does.

A man of faith once said, "I pray as if it all relies upon God, but then I get up and go and do it as if all relies upon me." To borrow from that very same concept as a leader, you should always support, encourage, and appreciate those in your team (upline and downline) as if it all relies upon them, but ultimately you must get up and go and do as if it all relies upon you.

## Self-Eliminating Leadership

The greatest challenge in developing leadership is you. It is a hard statement, but it is true. The hardest step to beginning that process is the first, and that first step is often not taken. This ensures failure. Not because of any other factor in life beyond a failure to even try.

In my late teens and early twenties I found myself living more than a thousand miles away from what I would call "home," in a small city called New Haven, Connecticut. An interesting fact about New Haven is that for the most part it is owned by Yale University, one of the premier Ivy League schools in the country. Students and professors in this community are considered some of the most brilliant people in the world, and they walked the streets of downtown New Haven every day. It was a remarkable experience to rub shoulders with people who I would never consider approaching in any other circumstance. See, I wasn't there to attend school, but I was there to fill a service role within the community.

In addition to not being there to attend school at this prestigious university, at this point in my life I was a high school dropout. I had dropped out in the tenth grade, and at that point had never looked back. It is not something that I am proud of, but not anything that I am ashamed of today either. Living in this environment in my early twenties changed my perspective on education, but one particular experience changed my perspective about my potential even more.

One day I was walking down the main street through Yale University, and I spotted a face that I recognized from my past life at home. It was one my drama teachers – actually probably one of the reasons I left school at such a young age. As a teacher, he was rather aloof, wasn't clear on most topics, frustrated students every day, and was probably not rehired the following year because no one enjoyed taking a class from him. When I saw him, I made a point to stop him and see what he was doing there at Yale.

He began to tell me that he was getting his Ph.D. in Theater Set

Design at Yale University. In one of those moments where your immediate reaction comes out, despite not being the most appropriate social response, I asked "How the hell did you get into Yale?"

Despite my candor, he taught me an important lesson that he probably doesn't even realize he left such an impact. He told me that he had applied for what the university referred to as a "Self-Eliminating Program." He said that there were a number of programs at these types of schools that have more openings than they do applicants, and that the only reason people don't apply is that they don't believe they could ever get into "Yale University." In essence, he told me that they eliminate themselves; not because they couldn't get into the program, but because they didn't believe they could – so they didn't even try.

I walked away from that conversation, and questioned immediately, "What am I self-eliminating myself from in life because I am not even trying?" Shortly after that I moved back home and enrolled in a state college that had open enrollment. Within four years, I earned my GED, my high school diploma, my Associate's as Valedictorian, and my Bachelor's as Summa Cum Laude – and was on my way to getting my MBA.

Too many of us self-eliminate ourselves from too many things in our lives, not because we can't do it, but because we don't even try. Leadership is one of those things. We don't see ourselves as a leader, and we may not be – but that doesn't mean we can't become one. The biggest trick to leadership is trying. Read, and apply what you are studying in this book – and see what you can learn to develop in yourself and your team. Don't let yourself fail, only because you didn't even attempt. That should be a general rule in every aspect of your life – from this day on.

## Leader of One

Before you can become an effective leader of many, you must learn to become a leader of one – yourself. Learning to lead is not about learning techniques or behavior about managing and inspiring others – it is first about learning techniques for managing yourself and your behavior. Only when you master yourself, may you be able to master others.

As you become a leader of yourself and learn the concepts within this section, you will find others gravitating towards your confidence and being willingly led by you. Leading others is not about persuasion or force, it is about others submitting themselves to your leadership and direction willingly because of their confidence in who you are and what you represent. There is no force in true leadership.

Others building confidence in you is based upon the confidence you build within yourself. This is based upon how you have become the leader of yourself. Building your temperance, exercising self-discipline, and genuinely becoming the person you wish others could be is critical to developing true leadership.

If you do not follow yourself, who will? If you do not believe in yourself, than who will? If you do not mold yourself into what you want to be, then who will believe you can help them reach a higher level themselves? This is ultimately the true goal of leadership.

To be frank, this takes work. And, if done right, you will be the most frustrating member of your team to be associated with. If you don't realize now that you are your own worst enemy in this business, then you do not know yourself well enough. To be the leader of one, you will need to focus on personal development, setting goals, and participating in honest and sincere evaluations (both by yourself and with others). You will not always like what you hear, or even what you feel about yourself at times. But to be a leader you will need to develop a level of honesty and transparency with yourself.

Seek to improve who you are, and further develop your skills and temperance. Seek to better understand what you want to do, and then train yourself to go and do it. There will be times when even you will disappoint yourself, but don't beat up on yourself too much! Just focus on being better today than you were yesterday.

Learning and developing the ability to be the leader of yourself will give you the discipline to succeed at everything you put your mind to. You will accomplish more than you ever dreamed you could! Others will look at you and want to be more like you; and therefore the potential to lead others will be born.

# You Are a Creator

Much of developing leadership is about a perspective change in who you are, who you can be, and a genuine belief in what others can become. One of the greatest perspective shifts that a growing leader can develop is the realization that they are a creator.

As a person, and as a leader, you move, act, and contribute to your environment in some form or fashion. From that action, the world or environment (including people) responds to that action, and something is created as a reaction. Sometimes it is a smile and sometimes it is frown. You can create a sale through your actions, generate offense, or fill the room with laughter. In a very real way, whatever reaction the world or your environment gives you, you had a direct hand in the creation of that result. You are a creator, you can change lives, and you create more than you currently now comprehend.

What you do matters to the world and the environment around you – and no greater reality exists. You have the power to act, and in turn, create. You can be a CREATOR of good things or bad things – but there is no avoiding it – you CREATE!

When you realize that, you are able to be more mindful of the actions that you take, and you may find yourself more considerate of your creations. You can create more smiles, more joy, and more happiness in the world.

One small example of this might be beneficial in order to understand the universal application of this in every action we take throughout our day.

While mentoring a leader of a growing organization, I was able to see this principle in action and the reality of its impact. This leader had never been a leader in anything before in her life, and she recently had found herself with a great deal of success in her organization (note the difference between success in an organization and leadership – because there is a difference). As my team and I were mentoring together on her leadership skills in an effort to help her manage this success and to inspire and create greater success, she mentioned to me that there was someone who seemed to have drifted from the fold. For one reason or another, despite the success this downline member had in her organization, it sounded like she was moving on and going to explore another opportunity. This leader didn't really know what to do about it, so I asked her to call this team member and talk with her. A few hours later this leader called me back, and relayed the following small details. When she had talked with this distant member of her team, it was confirmed that she was planning on working with another company. Nothing particularly negative in nature was said during the conversation on either end. When the phone conversation was over, this leader noticed on her social media stream that the downline member had suddenly posted a number of positive posts in relation to their company. As a result of her phone call, this leader had created something – positive social media posts, and possibly much more. This leader didn't write those positive social media posts herself, but she created them by starting a positive chain of events, with a simple phone call.

This was only a small example of the power you have to create. Every day as a leader you create feelings and emotions throughout your team. You have the power to create self-confidence and all of the actions that result as a consequence. You can create empowerment, happiness, comfort, and motivation. You also have the power to create devastation, disappointment, and frustration. Understanding this power of creation, is ultimately understanding your power and your personal responsibility. You are responsible for those things that you create. You can either create that which uplifts and edifies others, your teams, and your processes, or you have the power to destroy other's confidence in you, in themselves, and ultimately, your business. Your actions matter, because the consequences matter.

You are a creator, and that knowledge can help you be a remarkable force for good.

# Realize the Potential in Others

This concept is as simple as it sounds: Realize the potential in others is real. Even when others don't see it in themselves, knowing that they can achieve the same level of success and potential as you is critical. Leadership is about lifting others to become leaders themselves. It is about seeing something in others that they cannot see in themselves.

Often times people view leaders as bosses, tyrants, or those who are always pushing others down – but this is wrong. True leaders, who understanding the real formula for their own success, learn quickly that success is heavily relied upon the success of others. True leaders rejoice when people in their team succeed, and even more when they surpass them in title. Someone, who is afraid of losing their role as the leader, will always only lead the weak. The leaders who seek to elevate those they lead to be leaders themselves, will be leaders of the great. The strength of a leader is defined not by the number of people they "lead" but by the quality of the people they lead.

As a leader develops that potential in others, they ultimately see the fruits of duplication. They see the results of having more than just themselves working the business, and actually are able to experience the freedom that is so often promised but rarely received in this industry. This rare occurrence, however unfortunate the scarcity of it is, is not usually based upon a problem within the program or company they are working. Rather, it is based upon a problem in the internal programming of the "leaders." All leaders are given two options when it comes to developing leadership within their teams: (1) Develop others to succeed and become leaders themselves, or (2) "protect" their role as the leader and inhibit the growth and development of the team. Both approaches offer some financial success but only the first option can generate true freedom. The second option will only fulfill the supposed leader's pride and will ultimately lead to a co-dependent relationship with their organization. Thinking of the development of others will always give you a greater return than only focusing on the success of yourself. It was a good friend and significant earner in the industry who said, "I have learned that when I take care of others, I am taken care of; when their needs are met, mine are met; and when they succeed, I have succeeded."

# Part 2
# Development of One

RYAN DALEY

# The Importance of Developing Oneself

It stands to reason that learning to be a leader of one (you) requires learning to develop yourself first before you seek to develop anyone else. Your personal development will be the foundation for the level of development you can offer your team as a leader.

It is often said that in order for you to lift someone to a higher ground, you must first be on higher ground yourself. That is also true of leadership. People are not interested in following those who are on the same level with them – they want someone who can lift them higher. This higher ground relies heavily on your own personal development. Who you are, who you become, and who you are developing to be.

Your personal development as a leader is something that should never be a secondary priority. It has been a mantra of numerous companies in the industry that your priorities should be, "God, family, and your business" but if you are not present to say those words – such mantra is meaningless. Your personal development will be more valuable to you than anything else you can do as a leader. More importantly, your personal development as a leader will affect your development as a spouse, parent, neighbor, child, co-worker, or simply as a human being. If done correctly, your development as a leader will ultimately make you a better person. This makes your leadership development less about the end goal, and more about the development that takes place in your life through the process.

Remember you are the foundation of your soul, your action, and your reactions; therefore you are the foundation before any other priority can exist. You must excel first at self-development, before you can excel at anything else.

# Personal Development

Years ago the self-help section of the book store was an awkward place to be. Today it has been rebranded as "personal development" and contains some of the greatest books and bestsellers the publication industry has ever seen. This is because there is content out there that has changed lives and it has inspired people to achieve more than they previously dreamed of.

This section of the bookstore can be a great start on the road to personal development and self-improvement. Self-improvement is ultimately the goal; seeking to become a better person today in some way, than you were yesterday.

Go and discover the most recommended books in the category of personal development, and read them. More importantly, apply what you learn. As you read the words that have ultimately changed multiple lives and industries, you will find things that will inspire you to change. Then CHANGE! Apply those tidbits that inspire you and watch yourself become closer to the person that you want to be.

With this it should also be understood that there are more places than just books to work on self-improvement and personal development. There are seminars, lectures, modules, and other materials. The world is filled with quality information and knowledge on improving yourself and your behavior – there is no shortage.

Additionally, there is the study of one's faith or personal belief system. For those who carry a strong background or understanding of their faith, a regular study and application of those teachings can be the most powerful impact on personal development. Personal development is not about working towards becoming the person that others want you to be, it is about becoming the person that you want to be. If a person of faith is part of what you desire for yourself, than a study of that faith is critical to your personal development.

The world doesn't need more leaders like everyone else; they need one more leader like you.

## The Forever Student

The goal of personal development includes one more thing: The greatest leaders are "ever learning." They are constant students, at all times, and in all things. As a leader you will need to develop a habit of study, research, and gaining knowledge. This could sound boring and arduous, but is actually much easier than it sounds.

The fact is, if you were to spend thirty minutes every day dedicated to studying a single topic (consistently), you could easily be considered an authority on that topic. The great news is that in order to be a leader, you don't need to be an authority on anything. This gives you the ability to study many things over the course of your life. The key is consistent dedication to your continued education.

Take time every day and learn about your product or your services. When you have developed a comprehensive understanding, take some time and learn about your company, your industry, your compensation plan – truly immerse yourself, so that at all times you can speak with confidence.

You can also take thirty minutes every day and study topic related to your personal development, politics, government, religion, and anything else that you feel confident would help you develop a well-rounded education. This can be helpful and necessary as you seek to learn how to relate to others you come across, especially members of your team.

With all of this being said, this does not mean to just read something every day (although that would be better than nothing). This means to *study* something every day. Make a conscious effort for a period of time (days, months, years, etc.) to focus on one topic. Research it and develop a strong understanding of it. Be specific and very aware of what your goals are in your study and you will find yourself developing the habit of learning.

# Finding the Time

With the last two recommendations being "Personal Development" and "The Forever Student," the question should arise, "Where is the time?" Often times in leadership, the lack of desire to be a leader is not the issue. It is the time it takes to develop leadership that is the challenge. This is where true leaders quickly learn the power of time.

It was once said to me, "That what you spend your expendable time on, says a lot about where your priorities are." Every one of us has expendable time during the day. Whether it be two hours a day or only ten minutes a day, that time is there. This is time that we get to decide what to do with, because there are no bosses, there are no needs or requirements, and there is nothing forcing us to do anything specific during that time. It is what we do in those moments that speak volumes to our character and what our priorities are. It is in these times that what we choose to do with our expendable time (no matter how much or how little we have) that reflects which path we are on.

Do we spend that expendable time watching television, playing video games, or talking on the phone? Or do we spend it reading a book, studying our products, or planning the next business strategy we are going to implement? Are we hoping to be entertained for a few minutes of mental vacation? Or are we pondering upon the opportunities that are around us and how we might be able to take advantage of them?

A leader is mindful of this expendable time. They are always conscious of what they are doing during this time; making sure that they are building something with each available moment. To many leaders, this time is spent building their team, building their families, building themselves, or even their relationship with their God. Either way, they are building something with their spare time, and they are making sure that it reflects their priorities and values.

Using this expendable time is critical to your personal development and your goals as a student of the world; but identifying opportunities to create this expendable time is also a skill that can set leaders apart.

Each of us has time that may not be expendable time, but can be considered less effective time. This is time when we are driving in the car, exercising, traveling, or even standing in line at the grocery store. This is time where you are technically doing something, but you could be doing something more. Taking this time and being prepared to optimize this time can enhance your personal development and research goals significantly.

Get a few important books in audio format, and play them as you drive across town while you do your errands. You will be surprised to find just how quickly you can go through a book. Then listen to it again and again. Remember, repetition is the law of learning. You can also use this time in your car (pending you have hands free capability) to make phone calls to your team. I like to take this time and call through people that I might not otherwise stay in contact with. It makes the long trips go faster, and these conversation can maintain those relationships that will be more important in the future than you may now realize.

Get a few podcasts or mp3s on your player as you work out. You will not only be surprised with how much you can learn while you work out, you will be surprised with how quickly your body will grow accustomed to not working out with music. You will actually get a much better workout. I challenge you to do it for four weeks. You will be surprised at how much easier it is to stay consistent with a workout when you are not listening to music, but to something else.

Find ways to stay actively engaged in learning during unique times. There was a story that I once heard where a gentleman loved a book so much, that he would buy multiple copies of it, and then tear pages out of it and carry them around with him. When he would find himself in line somewhere, he would pull the page out and read it from front to back. When I heard this, I took the idea and starting to make small index cards with favorite quotes or lessons on them that I wanted to learn and memorize. When I would get stuck in line somewhere, I would pull them out of my pocket and review them or study them.

There are ways to maximize your time - especially that time that you currently think is filled. You will be surprised by how much time you actually have in the day to dedicate to your personal development study. Choose your expendable time wisely, learn how to maximize the rest of your time accordingly, and you will find your opportunities for development increase exponentially.

# Remain Teachable

Remember that everyone has something insightful to contribute. The ability for a leader to remain teachable is critical to their long term growth and success. Unfortunately, it is often the case that when someone builds a certain level of success, they come to the conclusion that they have achieved it based on their wealth of knowledge or their greater knowledge than another. This is usually a very shortsighted line of thought.

Your ability to remain teachable and continue to learn your trade, industry, and company program is the very act that will direct your success and future momentum. It can be seen every day when people assume that they have it figured out, and they actually stop progressing in their organization. Remain teachable at all phases of your organization, and your organization will always have an upswing potential. If you close it off, than you are telling yourself and your team that there is no more growth for you personally and in turn for the organization. This usually becomes an unspoken self-fulfilling prophecy.

This is not just a fluffy idea, but a fact of business. Even large companies that think they have it all "figured out" usually end up settling in too quickly. When the market changes, they are left behind, wondering what happened. This happens every day in this industry. As life and business remains fluid, those who anchor to their current knowledge base are eventually left in the waves.

This can be a difficult task based on your level of leadership. Remaining teachable is rooted in your ability to remain humble. Your ability to remain humble can be difficult as you develop yourself and continue to grow in your success. During your growth phases, there are times when people will praise you, the company will acknowledge you, and you will be surrounded at times with perspective-changing praise. It is within these times that the leader often falls into the gentle whispers of pride – and begins to agree with what is said about them. "Yes, I am good at what I do." "Yes, I am a great leader." "Yes, I do know what I am doing." These may be accurate statements, but often they feed into building a wall that makes them less teachable.

A small lesson that I learned more recently than I would like to admit, came in the form of a small story I heard. There was a man, who had been recently promoted into a position that had a significant amount of work involved. It also happened to be a highly public role. He would be working directly with the public, who would be elevating him, respecting him, and making extremely positive assumptions about him. They would be eagerly complementary, and would make sure that he would feel positive about their personal association. On his first public assignment, his supervisor traveled with him. As they drove in their car from the airport to their first of many, his supervisor (who had been in this situation for decades) leaned over and told him, "There is something you need to know. When you meet with them, they are going to complement you. They are going to praise you. They are going to make sure that you know that they respect, honor, and elevate you in their eyes. There is one piece of advice that I would like to give you. Let them do it, just don't breathe it in."

Remember that you are who you are. You are a person who was born like everyone else. You are just like everyone else in the way that you had to learn everything that you are doing - and that there is still more to learn. You inherently are not any better or worse than anyone else – but you are you. Let them praise you, let them build you up – as they need to create a leader to follow as well. You can – and should – let them do this. However, it is critical that you do not "breathe" it in. Remember that anyone who is willing to do what you have done, dedicate the time you have dedicated to it, and work as hard as you have worked can also achieve the same level of success. This fact should not be something that intimidates you, but should be the true foundation of building your business and your sense of leadership among your team.

## Seek to Be, Rather Than Find

One of the most common goals heard in the industry is the search for the perfect downline member. Everyone believes that if they find that one (or three) individual(s), they will have a great team, make a great check, and become a big leader in the industry (presumably with little or no effort required). This statement is somewhat rooted in fact and will be addressed in more detail later in this book. However, there are some underlying facts within this statement that should be evaluated.

There are people who have spent their entire career in Network Marketing looking for these "perfect" people - and they never find them. They spend their time looking for these individuals, and end up passing over the true potential that is within the imperfect people that they do find.

The greatest advice that has been given on this topic is, "seek not to find the perfect distributor – seek to become the perfect distributor." This simple advice has changed countless businesses from stalled to stallions.

Make a list for yourself everything you would love to see in your perfect downline member. Be honest about what you want other people to do and to be willing to do. This list might include: Being willing to talk with people, host parties, invite friends, invite strangers, listen to you (their upline), be nice, never get mad over unnecessary things, etc. It may even include more aggressive things: Be at every team meeting, attend every company convention, be on every webinar or conference call, and, in turn, get their team there, go on every incentive trip, and participate in every promotion. These can be lofty lists.

Then take that list, scratch out the top where it says "the perfect distributor downline member" and write "the perfect ME" on it. Take that list of everything that you want others to be, and work on becoming that yourself. Rather than search for the perfect

downline member, become that perfect member. When you do that
– you will find a huge paradigm shift in your organization, and a
pivot in your ability to lead by example.

You will find that your business will grow in ways that you
never thought of. You will find that you already found your perfect
distributor - YOU! You will discover that your team will achieve
more than even you thought they could, and that even more of them
will live closer to that standard that you yourself are living by. You
will ultimately get more out of them than you would have or could
have gotten any other way.

And here is the most interesting fact. You will begin to find
those leaders you are looking for! People who are true leaders (or
these perfect downline members that everyone is looking for) do not
sign up with other people who are not leaders themselves. Like
attracts like, and as you become more like the individuals you are
hoping to find – they will begin to grow closer to you naturally. They
will see your success, and your like-minded attitude, and they will be
more than willing to make it happen on your team with you. These
individuals will know they will be working with someone great, rather
than for someone "great" and there is a big difference between how
people respond to those two feelings.

You see, true leaders in the industry know the game. They
are not looking for an upline who is just going to mooch off of them.
They are looking for people who they can work with, because they
know that they will work with them and keep pace with them – if not
challenge their pace.

When you seek more to become that leader rather then find
that leader – your team will grow, you will grow, and those leaders
will find you!

# Your Environment

One of the most memorable quotes I have ever heard was given to me by an elderly mentor of mine:

*"Nothing touches the soul, but leaves its impress, and thus little by little we are fashioned into the image of all that we have seen, known, heard, and meditated. And if we learn to live with all the purest, the finest, and the best, the love of it all in the very end, will become our very lives." – Unknown Philosopher*

Everything that we surround ourselves with affects our life. The impact of our environment is possibly the most understated influence in our lives. What we have around us, makes us in ways that we cannot always comprehend. What we listen to affects us. What we watch forms our actions and our perception on the world. What we read molds our being, and who we surround ourselves with can help define our character.

Paying attention to our environment is key to developing who we are, and who we want to be. Listen to those things that uplift, edify, and raise you in a positive way towards what you want to become. Read books that make you aspire to be greater than you currently are. Watch programs that contribute to your life rather than numb your life. Surround yourself with beauty, positivity, and whatever the best may be. By doing this, the impact of these things will affect who you become.

Let me share a personal story that is a small example of the impact our environment may have, and how it can unnoticeably alter our actions, our future, and our behavior. As a student, I studied a wide spectrum in the behavioral sciences. The classic debate within psychology is whether personality and behavior is a result of nature verses nurture. I, of course, was more interested in the way people can change and alter their behavior for good, and so I was well aware of the behaviorists' theories that everything about us was based upon our environment. Although few swim in the deep end of those theories today, it is well accepted that there is a great deal that can affect our lives in relation to our environment. Needless to say, this was part of my study.

While I was in the middle of this study, my wife had decided to complete a project of her own. She created something that is known as a "dream board." This is something that is well-known in psychology, as well as within the industry – and I would recommend it to all (primarily because of what happened next). She began to search the internet and magazines for inspirational quotes, pictures of things she wanted to get, earn, or achieve, and in general she plastered her findings on a piece of poster board - making visual images of her hopes, dreams, and goals in life and throughout our marriage. To say that this was specific to her, was an understatement – this was very geared to her goals, rather than mine. When she completed the board, I thought it was cute as I had been aware of the theory for years, and she counseled me to do one myself. Not having reached the mature level of "application" from my research, I neglected to complete a similar project.

That dream board of my wife's got placed in the bedroom, right across from the bed near the master bathroom entrance. It was impossible to miss. Nearly every night before I went to bed I saw that dream board. Every morning I walked past it. Every day at least a few times a day it was in the corner of my eye. In those moments that my mind may have wandered from other things, I looked at the pictures, I read the quotes, and I knew everything that was on that board. Weeks turned to months, months turned to a year, and the poster board was fading from the light of the window.

One day I sat in bed with a laptop making a list of my goals for the next year, and the things that I had accomplished the year before (this was my version of goal making). As I was completing that list, I looked up at my wife's dream board, and then back at my accomplishments for the previous year. Suddenly I realized that without even noticing it, I was working down the path of her dreams on her dream board. Although, they were not my dreams, because they were in my face every day, there was something that propelled me in that direction. I was amazed at the genius it was for my wife to brainwash me that way! She was getting what she wanted in life because I was affected by my environment more than I would have ever imagined.

Be mindful of what is around you. Know the power that your environment has on you for good and for evil. Remove things from your life which you would not want to affect who you are and who you will become, and place things that will uplift and define your character in a positive way. Make dream boards of your hopes, dreams, and goals – and put it somewhere that you and your spouse can see every day. Even if your significant other doesn't want to participate, know that by putting it in their face (subtly) every day – they too can work towards your dreams without them even knowing.

Have good music and training material in the car as you drive – take time to read good material that will make you better. Know that what you spend your spare time on defines what your priorities are.

# Habits

The development of good habits is what creates consistent and reliable leaders.

A common theme in religious philosophy is to question why people are obedient to deity or in layman's terms why they do what they do. The most common theological answer comes in four stages. First, people are obedient out of fear – they are scared of what might happen if they don't obey. Then (second) they move to doing it because they will be blessed as a result of doing what they were doing. After that (third), they progress to a level where they do it despite blessings and cursing, but because it is philosophically "right." Finally (fourth), they reach a point where they do it because it becomes part of their nature. In multiple theologies, this is the stage at which man reaches his full potential – obedience out of habit or nature.

The path of leadership is very similar. We first do things because we are told to do them, and we might feel pressured to do so (either by society or our upline). We then (second) learn the rewards of doing these actions, and continue to do them because of the reward we get. Eventually, (third) we continue to do these actions because we know them to be "right" or part of the process of success. Then finally (fourth) these actions become habit, and perpetuate their success as a result.

As aspiring leaders, we learn things that we should do, and we do them. To stay consistent in doing what they know, leaders should eventually develop these techniques and characteristics into habits, building them into their nature. When something, whether it is an action or a characteristic become part of our nature, there is no longer an effort in the action – it just happens, because it is a part of us. This is where the concept of natural leaders (as mentioned in the first section of this book) is developed. These people appear to have natural skill. Not because they didn't work for it, but because they worked so hard for it. It became natural to them. These skills became habits. And these habits created, what looks on the outside to be, natural success, or effortless success. This is not to say that the success they earned was effortlessly done, just that the effort was put forth to generate these habits so much earlier that it became second nature.

It is our habits that ultimately will define who we are, and what we achieve in life. It is a sad comment to make, but true: Humans are the most malleable species on the earth. We are influenced more than any other creature, and have the greatest degree of changing that can take place as a result of our environment. We can be forcibly stubborn and avoid doing anything an authority figure openly wants from us, or we can somewhat ironically be subdued and submissive to a thirty-second commercial and blindly act upon the subconscious prompts made therein. This means that as humans, we are constantly in a state of change – whether subtly or openly. We are always growing or shrinking, thriving or dying, and the only way to minimize this reality is through the development of habits. In this constant ebb and flow we are always developing towards habits to minimalize this, even if we don't know it. The question is, what types of habits are we developing?

In this same vein of thought, we are either developing positive habits or negative habits at any given time. We are either reinforcing positive habits or weakening ourselves through the development of non-productive habits. The point is the development of positive habits does not just happen accidentally, while the development of bad habits happens without effort.

Good habits require focus, attention, and consistent behavior. They develop much like the development mentioned above. Leaders must identify an action that they want to be a habit, and then make a conscious effort to start doing it. They have to engage regularly until it becomes something that they enjoy.

Notice that the conversation is about doing some *until* you enjoy it. This breeds from the assumption that for the most part, the leader may not have enjoyed the action. As a leader you do not have to enjoy what you do, or some of the actions that you need to accomplish in order to find success; you just need to continue doing them. You are not paid, or rewarded as a leader because you only do the easy stuff; you are paid as a leader because you are willing to do the hard stuff. You are paid more than others, because you are willing to do more than others. Making these actions habits means that you have to do these actions, until you reach a point that you may actually eventually enjoy them, and from there, continue doing them until they become second nature. This will initially require any aspiring leader to step outside of their comfort zone, but eventually their comfort zone will realign with what they are doing and they will start enjoying the action, or at least the fruits of that action.

A common trick that is used when people are trying to get through the initial uncomfortable phase of leadership is the idea of "faking it until you make it." This sounds like a modern notion of hypocrisy, but in reality, it is a way for you to develop an appropriate respect for the actions that you are taking and eventually developing a love for. This is done by identifying an action that you know as a leader or builder of your team you should be doing, but may not enjoy doing. Then the next step is doing that action as if you love it, regardless of whether you do or not. Commit the action again and again, as if it is your favorite thing in the world. As this action continues, you will find yourself getting better and better at the action, and finding greater and greater success with it. Eventually you will find yourself enjoying it, and maybe even developing it into your nature.

# Money Magnifies

There is a small voice of warning that should be given here. Please realize that as leadership grows in this industry so does success. With success can bring greater wealth and money. With this being said, the need to develop personally throughout your leadership growth is even more important because money magnifies the person.

Money doesn't change you. It can't. What money does do is magnify who you already are by the time you earn the money.

This is seen in every circumstance where wealth is generated. When money is earned where it once wasn't present, you see a magnification of the personality traits that they carried with them at that time. Someone was a jerk before they had money; they become a bigger jerk with the money. If they were charitable and kind before the money, they become more thankful, humble, and charitable with the money.

There are times, when someone nice reaches a monetary milestone, and they seem to change in a negative way. This is not the case. What is more likely happening is that this negative part of their personality was there and present all along – they were just able to mask it socially. They were faking the positive aspects of their lives. Money just exacerbated the trait and made it more prevalent.

What this means is that it is critical for the leader to focus on themselves, not only for future success in their business, but for happiness in their lives. If a leader is unhappy before the money, the money will not make them happy. If they did not have positive attributes before their wealth, they will not develop those after their wealth. What you are today – in a very real way - is what you will be tomorrow, unless you consciously try to develop and improve who you are today.

Focusing on who you are and who you want to become before you find success, is critical to being able to enjoy the success in the future. Develop yourself so that when you find, earn, and build wealth, your true self can be magnified along with it, and you can be the type of leader that is respected in all walks of life.

# Part 3
# Leadership Building Philosophies

# Introducing Leadership Philosophies

Although there are numerous tactics for recruiting and building an organization, there is a great difference between the tactics themselves and the philosophies that under gird the potential success of a leader. It is critical for leaders within Network Marketing to understand some very important facts about the industry and team building that apply to everyone, in every company, and in every situation. Although these philosophies will not tell you exactly what you should do, they do define many concepts that you are virtually required to understand in order to create your own tactics and strategies correctly. If you can understand these concepts, it will aid in you creating a more cohesive building strategy within your respective company.

If you understand these concepts, it will help you have a clear perspective on the world of Network Marketing. The sections in this part of the book are not designed to be fluff or overly encouraging, but only to be factual on what you should expect as a leader. You try to lead and build within your organization. Understanding these concepts is like understanding the laws of nature – if you know them, you can use them to achieve significant goals. If you ignore them, you may always wonder why you can't jump to the moon.

## Like Attracts Like

There are numerous religions and worldly philosophies within the world, and you would be hard-pressed to find one that does not confirm on some level the notion that "like attracts like."

People like to be around people who are most like them. This could be seen as a form of human prideful arrogance, or it can be seen as a fact of life that can be used to create and generate success. Realizing that individuals enjoy being around people like themselves can help the leader define for themselves how people will be attracted to them in a working environment. This essentially dictates what type of person they themselves should be.

If a leader wants someone who is hard working, they need to be hard workers themselves. If a leader wants someone who is social, they need to work on their social skills. If a leader wants to attract other successful people, they need to learn to develop leadership and success within their own business.

Realizing this fact will help you manage your teams as well. As you look down into your organizations, you will begin to see little subsets of groups. These groups will be similar in mind and in activity. This is because they have been attracted to each other. In these subgroups within your organization, you may even find that they do not get along with other groups within your team; they may not even get along with you – the LEADER! Not only is this okay, it is natural. If they are attracted to work with another type of person, get out of the way and let them work with those who they feel most comfortable with! After all, they are still within your organization, and you will still benefit from their success. Sometimes the greatest leadership skill can be seen, not only in when to lead, but when to allow others to lead.

As a result of these subgroups forming, you will also notice that there will be members of these groups who do not feel comfortable working with the members of their own team. This is also okay, and natural, as they may not get along with them. It is entirely appropriate as a leader to help those within your team who seek your help, and who relate to who you are because "like attracts like."

Accepting this rule of the universe, as something that is known, will help you understand who you are attracting. This gives you an opportunity to adjust who you are attracting by adjusting who you are becoming through your personal development. If want to attract a different caliber of person, then you need to develop yourself into a different caliber of person.

Understanding this rule of nature will also help you understand the behavior within your organization. The degree upon which you understand human behavior will dictate how you respond to your team, and in turn how they respond to you.

# The Pipeline

The Pipeline is a concept that is used in the industry often, but is rarely understood accurately. "Filling the pipeline" has developed into a legendary concept for building a large and successful organization. However, through diluted word-of-mouth passing, we lose the true definition, explanation, and understanding of the original idea and it eventually loses all of its meaning.

When someone is referring to "the pipeline," they are referring to the fact that it takes time for people to develop and mature through the recruiting and enrollment process, and that leadership requires diligent and consistent effort and patience before one can see the fruits of it.

To explain the analogy of the pipeline, imagine for a moment that you had a twelve foot pipe (six inches in diameter), and that this pipe was on a slight angle. As you pour water through the top of the pipe, the water travels down the pipe and will eventually land at the bottom. This doesn't happen at the same time, nor does the same amount of water appear at the end of the pipe as was poured down.

If you are hesitant in building your business (pouring water down the pipe), you will want to test the water first. You will pour half a glass down the pipe, and then quickly look to see what comes out the other end. If you look too soon, you will find nothing. Consequently, you will quit pouring water, because you have neglected the time it takes to travel the pipe. At this stage, you may choose to walk away entirely. When that water appears on the other end, it will arrive with no one there to enjoy the fruit of it – and will evaporate. If you stick around long enough to see the water on the other end, you will realize that it finally arrived, rejoice in it – and then approach to go back to the start to pour more water.

In this analogy, the most effective approach is to continually pour water. Only then can you consistently have something coming out on the other end. If you stop pouring on one end, it will eventually stop appearing on the other end; although it may take some time to put this pattern together.

In building your business, the term "filling the pipeline" means that you continually work at putting people on the path of joining your team, knowing that it take times. It means that you understand that the difference between your effort and your harvest is delayed, and that you do not get disappointed or discouraged because of that. This requires you to stay consistent in your efforts, knowing that success will eventually appear, and knowing that once you stop, you will need to restart at a later date if you choose to reengage.

As a leader understanding this principle, or at least the concept of delayed results, is critical to your continued success in your team. Teaching this principle to your organization will help them understand the big picture between their efforts and the harvest that they expect. It will help explain why businesses slow down (including yours) – as there may have been a pause in filling the top of the pipeline. It will also help you understand why they stop altogether when everything else seemed to be going well.

## The Harvest and The Planting

Related to the concept of the pipeline, is the concept of harvesting and planting.

As leaders begin to grow their business, they work hard at building recruits and enrolling new members of their team. This activity seems to the main focal point in those critical growth stages. Then at some point in a leader's business, they see that their organization is large, seems to be stable or growing, and that there are other leaders developing or revealing themselves within the organization.

For whatever reason, at this stage the activity that was so critical to the growth of the leader's organization seems to slow down. They start to focus on developing their leaders, and helping them grow to higher levels. This often takes place with the correct understanding that the more these team members succeed, ultimately the more the leader will succeed. In many respects, this is considered "the harvest."

The harvest begins to take place when the leader looks at their organization and realizes, or thinks, that they have two options: (1) they could go and work on recruiting another few people, and increase their volume minimally in relation to their total volume, or (2) they could go work with their new leaders; building each of them to higher ground with the understanding that as these individuals grow, it will allow the leader to become a higher-ranking distributor. Presented with these two options, the leaders decide to do the latter, and "harvest" their current leadership to help themselves rank advance or grow to the next level.

Understanding the full scope of this principle, and why that is not exactly what should be done, is difficult for many leaders because of the sound foundation upon which the decision was made. It is true that if they go and "plant" or recruit more people in the short term it only incrementally increases their volume by small amounts (in comparison). It is true that they will grow more quickly with additionally increased volume by working with their leaders. It is also true that the more successful the team members are, the more successful the leader will be. There really is nothing wrong with the action that is taken in working directly with your current team members to help them succeed. What makes understanding this principle for leadership difficult is there is nothing wrong with the course of action taken in the example above. Additionally, there is nothing wrong with the logic used to come to that determination.

The principle of the harvest and the planting, is found in the error of ONLY doing one of those two things. Leadership in this principle is not about "options" between two mutually exclusive actions. Leadership in this principle is about understanding the importance and impact of not selecting one or the other, but of finding ways and times to do BOTH activities. A short-sighted leader will only harvest, and then when the harvesting is done, will stall and plateau in their organization. However, the leader that seeks for continual growth within their own organization knows that after the harvest – if something isn't already in the ground to grow, when the time comes for something else to be harvested, there is nothing there to work with.

The principle is this: No matter where a leader is at in their business size, if they are not planting new seeds, enrolling new team members, or personally building their business, when their current leaders matures, they will be stalled, or dammed like a river of water from progressing. As one harvest season ends, another already needs to be in the middle of its development. A leader must always be working with their current leadership to help that generation grow to its potential, while at the same time planting and nurturing the next generation to be harvested at a later date.

Even though the immediate increase in your organization is minimal with these new small plants, as they grow they will become a more significant factor in your organization for the next harvest season. This is the only way to develop a long term, continually growing business.

# Finding the Three (or the Three Hundred)

There is a common statement, based on fact, that is circulated in the industry and often misunderstood. It is when some leader makes the statement that they really make most of their money from no more than three members of their team. This concept is seen in the attempts to duplicate it among a population in their team. It creates the illusion that one only needs to only enroll two or three people, and then to help them enroll two or three people.

In theory, these statements are correct. But in application and reality, there are two important things that the true leaders needs to understand.

First, there is a time and a place to teach a simplified duplication model, such as only enrolling two or three people within a person's team. This simplified duplication model should not be taught because you genuinely believe that this has the greatest potential – because it doesn't. What it does do is serve as a reasonable means to get more out of your team than you otherwise wouldn't have received.

This means that most people don't enroll two to three people in their organization. For most people being told the simplified version of their potential (which philosophically speaking may be true), it may inspire those people to do more than they otherwise wouldn't have done. This can be an appropriate method; however, this is not the true path of leadership, only a marketable slogan to get the 99% to some form of action. The second point must be understood by the true leader – and taught to those in their organization who are true leaders.

Second, the reality is that it takes masses to find the few that will generate you your wealth. Yes, for most leaders they make the most from only a few. But the reality is, without enrolling the masses they would have never found those few. You must enroll hundreds of people to find the one or two that will meet or beat you at your own game – and, in turn, make you a fortune.

It may be a nice philosophy for the masses that they only need to enroll two to three people to generate some success; but the true leader knows that they need to be continually enrolling to find the three or four that will make them millions.

Realistically speaking, it takes an average of 100 enrollments to find someone who will match you in your activity. This means that in order to find the three, four, or eight you need within your company that will put you on easy street, you will need to multiply that number by 100 (300, 400, and 800). That is the amount of people you will need to enroll to reach critical mass in this industry.

If that makes your heart sink – remember that this is not to say that you cannot generate success. We are only talking about facts. In between where you are today, and where you could be there is a happy medium that may take less effort or require a smaller number. But the facts of life mean that it will not be the same level success it would be if you had enrolled those larger numbers. Remember, you don't have to be a billionaire to be happy with your organization – but don't expect to be one if you don't put in the same effort required to be one.

It should also be noted that if there is something about this that truly discourages you, than I apologize. Maybe being a leader in this industry isn't for you. Maybe the success you can develop by enrolling the two or three people is satisfactory to you. If it is, than bless you in your endeavor. The object of this section is not to convince you to do something that you do not want to do; it is only to explain the reality of the industry that you have to understand in order to have a clear perspective on what you need to do to reach those heights.

# Understanding Momentum

Momentum is another word that is used in the industry by more people than who know what it actually means. It sounds fun, fast, and important – and so it is spoken of like it means something to most people. The reality is, if you don't know what momentum, is then it doesn't mean anything to you. Even worse, if you don't know how to create it, then you don't know how to use it or focus on it.

The reality is momentum is the single most important thing a leader can know how to work towards. This is because real leaders don't care about checks, enrollments, downline growth, or any of these arbitrary numbers. They focus on momentum because they know that if they focus on momentum, everything else falls into place. They understand that check sizes, enrollments, and downline growth are not the goal, they are the result of the goal. They are the consequence of what happens, not what happens in and of itself. Momentum creates large checks, fast growing organizations, and everything that people search for. Whereas, focusing on the result (big check) rather than the formula (momentum), will leave them with their wheels spinning fast with no traction.

Mathematically speaking, momentum is a product of mass (size) and velocity (speed), and is related not to how fast something is going, but how much faster it is going at one point than it was at another. In your organization, momentum is a type of energy that is connected with the size of your organization and the speed upon which your organization grows. Note that it is an ENERGY within your team; an excitement toward action. It happens when you have groups of people moving in the same positive direction (the larger the group or mass, the larger the velocity). It is about creating a message and direction for this body of people to follow, to focus on, and adhere to. As the body of people move and act, they create momentum, adding to their numbers and increase their masses. It increases in speed and size – and therefore creates momentum. It moves faster and faster, growing larger and larger. As a consequence, it produces the numbers that everyone else thinks they should be looking for (checks, enrollments, etc.). But the member of the team who focuses on numbers, never achieves what they are looking for. The leader who focuses on momentum, places their efforts on creating something that will generate every number they could have wanted and then some.

As a leader, you must focus on creating this energy within your team. This is created by working directly with the members of your team, and helping to create a unity (as much as possible) in the direction they are going. Creating excitement and genuine enthusiasm for your business and what you are doing is a great step! Teaching your team how to do the same, and to create that energy in their own teams. THIS IS YOUR GOAL AS A LEADER! There is no more important goal than this! Momentum, momentum, momentum.

## Applying, Teaching, and Training on Momentum

Momentum may be a concept that is a highly misunderstood, but the creation of it is actually rather simple to teach. To create momentum, you and your team must do something positive more often than you do something negative. This concept of momentum applies to nearly everything in life, and once the idea is understood and it is applied to everything it is more easily applied in your business.

For instance, let's use this basic concept of momentum with something simple, to see how it applies.

Imagine you decided you wanted to weight lift. If you lifted weights four days out of seven days every week, you will have momentum in your weight lifting. This is because you are lifting weights more days than you are not. Those weeks that you might take a break or even lift only three out of seven days, you have zero momentum (or negative momentum). Momentum happens the moment you are doing one thing more often than you are not doing it.

Now, in this analogy it should be noted that there is a difference between a little momentum and a lot of momentum. Take the analogy above: There is a significant difference in the momentum that is experienced between lifting six days a week compared to only the four days a week.

You can do something 51% of the time and create momentum. But it will only be small in comparison to what you might see at 55%, 60%, 75%, or 90% of the time!

Momentum compounds upon itself, increasing upon its mass and speed, to becomes larger and larger, as it moves faster and faster.

Although this explanation of momentum is simple and brief, it should be enough to start the leader at any level in their business down the path of understanding the impact that teaching and training momentum can have on their business.

# JUST GO, APPLY, AND DO IT!

The single most significant attribute that sets a leader apart from someone who is not, is their ability to apply principles they learn. As you read, study, listen, and seek out knowledge, you will gain helpful insights in building your business, increasing your income, and developing stronger relationships with your family and others you come in contact with. The value of gathering this information is not so that you can have it, but so that you can apply it.

We live in a world where we value the valueless. We value having the knowledge, but not as much the application of that information. We have created a society where we accept that application is difficult, and therefore somehow knowledge is an acceptable replacement.

The most important attribute a leader can have is their ability to go and do it! To not only read and gain knowledge, but to apply that knowledge.

Throughout your leadership lifespan within your organization, you will witness countless trainings, and gain immeasurable amounts of information as to how to better grow your business. This information is worthless if you do not go and apply it. Make it a simple rule, that when you learn, you will go and do.

This might sound too simple, or even common knowledge – and it might be. Unfortunately, it is not common application. If you know that by doing three calls a day you can build a business, then do three calls a day. If you know that passing out thirty business cards a week builds your business, then do it. If you know that hosting team meetings strengthens your organization then host those meetings.

It is the simplest and still the hardest rule to follow. This is because at times the things that we know we should be doing are sometimes uncomfortable for us to do (at least initially).

Let me share with you an example, and let's see if this can help.

Earlier in my career, I knew there was one fact about my business:

Making phone calls helped. I also knew something else about phone calls: That I hated doing them. Phone calls make me feel uncomfortable, as it seemed to be somewhat of an unknown. I would often sit and procrastinate making those calls. I would make my to-do-list for the day, and put phone calls right at the bottom. I would wait until there was absolutely nothing left to do but make those calls before I did them. I cringed all day awaiting them.

Then one day I got to work, and there was nothing to do at all but make those calls. I had no more excuses. I looked down at the phone, and I just decided – I WAS JUST GOING TO DO IT. I decided to put my concerns aside and just get it done. I was triumphant for that day, and it wasn't as bad as I thought it was.

Even when I realized that it wasn't as bad as I thought, and that those calls were actually the most important thing for me to do for my business, it still didn't change how I prioritized my day. I was still putting them on the bottom of my list. Eventually I realized that this wasn't working as well as I had hoped for my business. I decided to take a different approach to my to-do-list. I decided to put what I hated doing at the top, and leave my favorite stuff at the bottom. This decision changed my life.

Doing this forced me to get through the "worst" part of the day first, while feeling better about what was to come. It also made me realize that if I just did what I knew I was supposed to do, it would actually get done, my business would grow, and things would be better.

Often times in life, the things that are the hardest are actually the most important things that need to be done. So it is in business. When lessons are learned, and things need to get done – commit to yourself to just do it – apply it- and make sure things happen! This is the way that leaders develop.

# Repetition

There comes a time as a leader when you have heard your message, your model, and your approach time and time again. You can get bored, or overcompensate in other areas because you no longer feel your words are relevant to you anymore - and maybe to anyone else.

Remember that repetition is the law of learning. Your comments, lessons, and message may no longer be relevant to you in your personal life. These may be skills you have perfected and refined, and therefore would love to move on from. But remember, there are others on your team who haven't heard those messages, lessons, or the basics yet. Don't get bogged down with the thought, "I have taught this already. I have already done this webinar. Why am I just talking about the same thing over and over again?"

Even more important, there are people who may have heard the message but have never really received it. Humans need to hear something over and over again before they really get it. You need to remember that your team is the same way. You need to be repetitive in your message. You need to let them know over and over again what you expect from them, that they can do it, and what it will take. They need the constant motivation, but they also need the constant reminder of the fundamentals of your business. Always assume when you are teaching your team that you are teaching the new person the fundamentals, even if they have heard it a million times already. Only when you have identified leadership in those who have listened a million times and have perfected the fundamentals, are you able to move off of the repetitive message. From there you can move on to the slightly less repetitive messages.

# Common Denominator

A leader in this industry is skilled in not only being able to find what they are looking for in people, but being able to know what they are looking for in people. They are able to look through the haze and fog of the expectations of the world, and see through to what they are really looking for.

When leaders look to find new members of their team, they do not look for those who are successful in their lives, or who seem like they would be 'naturals.' They are not looking for people who are unsuccessful in their lives, or who seem like they could grow into the role. They don't look for anything as arbitrary as a skill set or a history in one direction or another – they look for the least common denominator.

There is something that is at the core of all successful leaders and people within this industry, and that is what they are looking for. Next time you are in the room with your team, look around and try to see what the least common denominator is among them. You will see school teachers and bankers, you will see "A" students and drop outs, and you will see people with a strong family background and others with broken homes. None of these aspects of their lives dictate their potential for success. The common denominator in that room is dissatisfaction with some aspect of their life. Whether it is a frustration with finances, health, or their socioeconomic impact in their community – there is something which each networker is ultimately dissatisfied with. That is what you as a leader are looking for.

There are people that you will come across who could make millions, they could be naturals in the industry, and do much good – but if they are not dissatisfied with some aspect of life, then they are not looking for anything more. They could be amazing, but they won't have enough drive or desire for something to change in their life to make it happen.

That is what you are looking for! Regardless of any other aspect in their lives, you are looking for a desire and drive to change something. That is something that you cannot teach or train someone to have. The common denominator among every successful networker is a dissatisfaction with some aspect of their life.

As that simple fact is identified, a leader is able to first find and identify their potential team members more easily – and then second, tailor their message more effectively. If you are looking for dissatisfied people, you can find them. When you find them, you need to identify what they are dissatisfied with, and then have something to offer them that will resolve that need in their lives.

# Part 4
# Leadership Perspective

RYAN DALEY

# Managing Your Perspective – True Key to Success

Managing your perspective as a leader is critical to how you react to the world, and how the world (and your team) reacts to you. Keeping your perspective not only accurate, but positive and insightful will be the way you keep your team and yourself moving in a positive direction.

More importantly, to become a leader, your perspective will be the greatest barrier to your success in that goal. Within Network Marketing, your company, the opportunity you present, and even within your team, there is a great potential in front of you to do remarkable things. Just like the self-eliminating leaders discussed in the first part of this book, the greatest challenge to overcome will be yourself - and that is directly tied to the perspective that you allow yourself to carry with you. There are sections within this part that should help align your perspective with what your goals and potential may be, and help you reach to higher ground. This takes an honest degree of self-introspection that may not be comfortable for everyone, but it isn't designed to be.

There are times when your perspective will shift, and that will be felt within yourself. At those moments, it can require some time to step back and realign yourself with your goals, ideals, and values as a leader. Managing your perspective as a leader is just as much about gaining control of yourself and your thoughts as it is about helping your team. You need to become the master of your domain, your vision, and therefore your future – and that can only be defined by how you see the world and respond to that perspective. The reality of the world is not what we see, or even how it is; it is how we perceive it to be.

It is important that your perspective is based on facts and reality, as well as potential. It is important to remember how long some things can take. Within every process there are ebbs and flows, and that foundation to your perspective is key to being able to accept those peaks and valleys with a grin; knowing that one must follow the other. As long as the progressive moment is upward, success is guaranteed.

## The Cut of Leadership

The "cuts" of leadership are aspects of being a leader that could hurt. They are naturally occurring, and will happen to everyone at some point or another as their organization grows. These are eventually unavoidable.

As a leader you cannot make everyone happy within your organization, nor will you appeal to everyone. There will be people who just will not like you. This will not be because you have done anything wrong (although sometimes it is), but it may be because of how people perceive you and the assumptions they make about your success. We live in a world of jealously, pride, contention, and fear.

The first thing you must consider within this "cut" of leadership is that you cannot expect everyone to like you. There will be complaints about you, arguments about your style of teaching, and even people who would wish never to talk with you. This is okay and even normal. Make sure that you do not let it eat at you, and that it doesn't stop you from continuing on a path that you are confident will generate you greater success.

As mentioned earlier, when there are people in your organization that do not like you, but are finding a form of success in their business, get out of their way and do not take it personally. They are still making you money, and they are still finding success. Do everything you can to encourage them in their way of building their business. Keep in mind that might include not being involved with them at all. If they don't want to like you, but make you money, you let them keep going. Don't let your pride get in the way of your own success through them. It is a favorite statement of success that "I would rather be rich than right (about an argument)." It lends the same idea here – that as leaders you would rather be more successful than liked by everyone who is making you successful.

The second "cut" of leadership is the reality that within every complaint there is an ounce of truth. There was a wise man that once taught this concept: When someone complains about you, no matter how wrong they are, or how exaggerated the concept is, there is something that you have done to instill that seed of thought within their mind. There is some action that planted the seed, or some small ounce of truth to it.

These truths (or cuts) require the leader to find the balance between not taking complaints personally, and not being totally deaf to them either. This balance is found by not taking these issues personally, but in finding time when emotions can be put aside, and sincere self-evaluation can take place where it is asked, "What may I have done to plant that seed?"

There are times when we have done something – in fact most of the time. Yet, the interesting key here is that even if you have done something to plant that seed, the next question is whether that means that you should do something about it or not. There are many times when indeed you can identify what you have done, but there is nothing that needs to be changed; as it was in the best interest of your goals, your team, your family, or something else of greater value. It is okay to say, "I see where they may think that – but I would make the same decision again."

Then there are times of true growth, when the realization takes place of the small seed that was planted unnecessarily which started that issue. This gives each leader the opportunity for self-development and growth. This is the chance to find within yourself your next personal goals and develop into a greater leader. This is a time to evaluate what you could do to fix the issue, and take the necessary steps.

Part of being a leader and building a strong organization is realizing that contention is not always a bad thing. Issues give you opportunities for growth. When a muscle is worked hard, it develops small tears in the tissue, which are eventually filled in with more muscle creating a stronger structure. This is much like our organizations. There are times when contentions may arise, and cuts or tears may be generated. How you respond in these moments will either strengthen your team or weaken it. Is there something you can do to strengthen your team in these moments? If there is, do it! Take the opportunity to correct the issues, learn from the mistake and strengthen your team members in the process.

Leadership can hurt, and it is not always easy – but it is always worth it.

RYAN DALEY

# Defined by Your Success NOT Your Failure

One of the most difficult things for a developing leader to do is to define their perception by their successes rather than their failures. This is an important tool that each leader must develop.

Often times this fact is the defining line between a leader continuing on and growing to greater success, or giving up and dropping the success that they once had or potentially could have had.

This is often seen, not only in yourself, but within your organization, when someone evaluates not what they have accomplished, but what they haven't accomplished. There are too many potentially successful leaders in the industry who are new to the industry, who look at their $500 check in their company and are frustrated that it is not $5,000 – and they quit. They neglect the fact that they have achieved $500, and that once they have earned their first $500, they now know how to make the second $500, and so on to success. They forget about what they have achieved, and are focusing on what they haven't achieved.

When we are discouraged, or we feel that our team members are discouraged about not having accomplished certain goals, we need to learn to stop and teach. Take a step back and look behind us at just how far we have traveled. Take those moments not to feel sorrow for the unaccomplished, but rejoice in all that has been accomplished. The road has been traveled, successes have been made – and as much as there is more to come, each individual should learn the ability to feel confidence in that which they have been able to accomplish already. There are small successes all throughout your organization that if nurtured properly, will propel people to higher levels than they ever believed possible.

By being able to look at your successes rather than your failures, you have a better perspective to look at where you could be if you continue on.

RYAN DALEY

# Manage Your "Arrival" and "Why Is My Business Stalled?"

Every leader, or distributor, in this industry has a point of "Arrival." This is where they realize that they have arrived at their leadership role, and have accomplished something significant for their business in the industry. For each distributor or leader in the industry, this is defined by different things, and is often something that naturally happened within their organization.

This realization of "arrival" is one of the most devastating things to the growth of that leader's organization because it changes their perspective and therefore, adjusts their future potential in a detrimental way. When someone develops the perception that they have arrived, they stop listening to others, stop learning, and stop growing. Humility and teach-ability dissolve, and they expect things from the company that they didn't expect before. They grow content with their successes rather than seek new challenges. They place a subconscious ceiling on their success, and inevitably live up to the limitations that they place on themselves. Unfortunately every leader eventually "arrives," and when it happens, everything changes. As their perspective changes, they begin to wonder why their team is not responding to them the same way, or why the company may not be as responsive or positive about their association.

Not realizing that their perspective has changed, this can be the subtle shark in the water that stalls their business.

Now, here is the scariest part: Everyone experiences this at a different level. There are leaders who earn a million dollars a year before they "arrive," and then there are those distributors who earn only $300 in their check and decide that they have arrived. This is the challenge because it is different for each person. If you don't see it in yourself, you should look at your organization to realize this fact. There are people who grew quickly to $300 but can't seem to work anymore to grow any further. This is because that is when they "arrived." They subconsciously viewed that as their ceiling of success. They may even be surprised that they were able to achieve that success and therefore don't believe that they can achieve more. Some in your team may make $5,000 a month, and suddenly cannot grow any further. They seem to have had an attitude change, and wonder why people are not responding to them. They are not listening to the company, and think they have developed a better way that doesn't seem to be nearly as successful. As you see this, realize that this is a reality within yourself as well. Many of these people don't see it in themselves, nor would you see it in yourself unless it was pointed out. Consider yourself pointed to!

Managing your arrival is critical to not prematurely stunting your success. Being able to identify that this process is happening in yourself and your organization is the first step to combatting it. When it comes to others, you may have problems teaching them to avoid it – but when it comes to yourself, the occasional gut-check is important. Ask yourself the following questions:

- Am I changing the way I have built my business?
- Has my business suddenly slowed?
- Do I no longer believer doing certain acts are necessary for my business, even when it's been proven that they have worked for me in the past?
- Am I teaching others to do things that I am no longer willing to do myself?
- Have I suddenly stopped listening to those who I had listened to while building my success (upline, sponsors, or even corporate staff)?
- Do I feel that the company owes me something?

If you answered yes to any of these questions, you may want to take stock as to whether or not your slowed growth is because you have "arrived." When this happens, resetting yourself to the basics of your organization is an immediate and important act that must happen. Reconnecting with your team, reengaging with the basics of the program as if you were a new member of your team yourself, and getting back into what you know you should be doing is critical. Realize that the new things you are doing that may seem easier now, might not actually work. Then jump back to those things that do work.

The most common question asked of those who work closely with developing powerful leaders in Network Marketing is "Why has my business stalled?" The response is often based on the fact that the individual has reached their personal arrival: "Why has your business stalled?"

This usually creates a great deal of frustration with the leader – and it is intentional. The follow up question that is asked of the leader is "What are you doing differently today that you were or were not doing when your business was growing?"

Depending on how far into the their arrived stage the leader is at will determine how long this conversation will go. For some truly introspective leaders, they will be able to take some time and respond to a number of small, but important things, that they were doing at the beginning of their business that they are no longer doing. They can quickly learn the need to get back to basics and start building as before.

On the other hand, some individuals can take some prodding; but as long as they stick with it they will eventually discover what some of those steps were. In these conversations, the challenge can get heated as the question keeps coming: "What are you doing differently?" Sometimes it is necessary to remind them of a simple fact before they can take the exercise seriously. "When your results changed so did your behavior. What behavior has changed that has altered your results?" This should be a question that any "stalled" leader should ask themselves – and you don't need a coach to do it.

Get a spouse or partner, and have them ask the question. If needed, have them ask you the question over and over again until you finally get a list of things you did. Write down everything you can think of - large or small - that you are doing differently now than you were when your business was growing. Don't let this person go easy on you. Make them force you to think through the entire process.

A common response in this activity is, "I don't know." This is a sign that you have undervalued the simple processes of the business. There are small things that you did that really were not as small or insignificant as you thought they were. You undervalued your activity. That means that in this process, you have to then focus on those small, seemingly insignificant actions that may have been great keys to your success. You can tell you are starting to hit the mother-load of these important items when you hear yourself say, "All I did was…" Those words are indicators that you did in fact, do something differently; that you undervalued those actions (and still do), and that they are exactly the steps you need to reintroduce to get your business moving again.

When this list is completed, evaluate it, and then apply it. If you look at this list and are no longer interested or willing to do those actions, then your business has not stalled – you have. There is no other blame to place. If you are truly dedicated to leadership, your team, and your future, then you will take that list, humble yourself, and begin anew. Start to apply them, and watch your business begin to grow again.

Manage your "arrival" and teach others to manager theirs. Take stock of your own actions when you feel your business has slowed, and then reset to the basics that built your business. Teach others to do the same.

## Never Judge Others' Potential

If there is anything within this industry that most people, including leaders, mistakenly do it is to judge others' potential within their organization or within Network Marketing. This can be something that is all too easy to do. When we see someone who walks into our party, or our meeting, and they may not have groomed properly for the day, or they may have to pay you with small bills and change, it is easy for us to assume that this might not be the right business for them. Sometimes we learn about someone on welfare, or needing to borrow money from a relative to get started, and we think that they might not be thinking clearly. We can easily make assumptions as to whether someone can or will succeed within this industry.

Interestingly enough, this truth goes both ways. There are times when we meet someone and we assume that they are perfect for our team. We get genuinely excited about their potential and make the opposite assumptions: These people are going to hit it out of the park.

Both of these assumptions are wrong to do, and will hamper the progress of your organization.

Let me relate two quick examples of this happening, and please keep in mind that these are not exceptional examples – this takes place every day.

Early in my career, I was managing some leadership fly-ins for a company. They were bringing their leadership in for a summit. One of the leaders had requested an extra ticket for someone who they were signing up who was going to be a "rock star." We were allowing each leader to bring one guest, and so we approved the extra ticket. That weekend, I met this individual and he impressed me. He was well spoken, smart, and seemed to get the hang of things quickly. He talked the talk, and as much as I could tell, this leader was right – he was going to be remarkable.

That same weekend, I met with the guest of another leader. This middle-age woman told me that she lived in a trailer park, was having trouble paying her bills, and that she wasn't "good with people." Talking to her made me nervous, and I began to get a small feeling of guilt bubble up inside. I wondered how I felt ethically about encouraging her to sign up and spend over $300 to get started knowing that she was struggling.

At the conclusion of that weekend, both guests signed up with the company. By the end of the month, the gentleman who impressed us so much had reached a preliminary leadership rank and we were so very proud. But by the end of the second month, he had all but quit the company; not for any reason in particular, he had just felt it was time to not do it anymore.

A few months later, I started to hear someone's name pop up in casual conversations about growing leadership. The name seemed familiar, and I eventually realized that this new growing leader was the very woman whom I had all but dismissed. Within a few months, she had grown her organization and check to a level where she was making a significant income, and had surpassed in rank the "rock star" we were all so sure of months before. I then realized that if I had been the potential sponsor to her, I probably wouldn't have even given her the time of day. I would have made the decision for her by not letting her register and start the business.

Experiences like this happen every day in this industry. Lives change, and people change. As leaders we need to recognize that and allow everyone the opportunity to change the direction of their path. We need to make sure that we do not judge others' potential or future success, but let them make those decisions for themselves.

This leadership trait will serve you well for a number of reasons. Your organization will grow stronger as you encourage everyone to join in an attempt to help them reach their full potential - regardless of where they currently are in life. The members of your team will achieve more as you show them your confidence and belief in who they are and the potential of who they can become. For many people, this will be the first time they may have someone exercise faith in them. Finally, it makes your job as an enrolling leader easier, as you don't have to take it upon yourself to judge or make judgment calls for others – your role is to give others an opportunity, and let them accept it or reject it themselves.

Within the earlier example, there is another lesson to learn. When a leader goes out into the world to find members of their team, there is a common error that takes place. This is the desire to find those "rock stars" to join the team. The leader goes into the world with what he imagines is the perfect person to join his team, and overlooks all of the imperfect people. Sometimes this term is also called "whale hunting." It is when leaders only look for the big hitters to join their team, and ignore all the small fish that have all of the real potential to grow.

## Managing Personal-Professional Relationships

This industry carries with it a constant challenge of learning the balance between professional and personal relationships. This is because your business is so involved in the lives of others. Success is found in the ability to relate, communicate, and learning to help real people. There is a portion of your business that is very connected to building relationships of trust and learning how to listen and respond to people in a very genuine way.

In addition to these realities, as a leader builds their team they need to be able to lead, train, and inspire on a personal level. People often need to feel connected with members of their team and upline to be influenced in a positive way, and this can lead to a need to develop personal relationships with members of our downline. This enmeshment of personal relationships with members of our business team, can not only feel natural at the start of your business, but almost necessary. However, this perspective can often lead to a number of very real complications that make it even more crucial for true leaders to learn a proper balance and perspective in the relationships and boundaries they have with members of their team.

These personal relationships can actually be frustrating, hurtful, and detrimental to leaders over time. As there are two parties in each relationship, each party may value the personal relationship on a different level. Even more difficult, is when each party treats personal relationships in different ways with different behavior. Remember that each person is a collection of experiences, environment, and choices that they make in life; and their definitions, actions, and what is determined as appropriate behavior in any type of relationship can be something very different than another. This can lead to personal frustration, and a very real threat to the longevity of your business, when the endurance requirements that are placed on true leaders in the industry begin to present themselves.

For example, when one party lets down their guard within a

personal relationship with a team member, and the other party takes some personal information and spreads it around – that personal relationship can be in jeopardy as the offended party reacts. And yet the member "in the wrong" here sees nothing unique about their actions, as it is normal within their defined understanding of appropriate behavior within their relationships. This can also be seen when personal relationships are misinterpreted to be closer than they might actually be between two parties, or representations are made by one party about the feelings, intentions, and motivations of another party. Personal relationships among team members can create opportunities wherein small offenses become engorged, and can become much larger issues than they normally would. Take for instance, the team member who thinks that the personal relationship she had with a team member is so strong, but she doesn't get a phone call back from the message she left. For some reason she is offended and feels rejected by the action (or lack of action), even though no ill was intended. All of these types of conflict yield no positive result. They generate distractions within the team that slow its progress, and places other people (including the leader) into activities that waste time, that otherwise could have been focused on the more productive behavior of building, nurturing, and recruiting.

These are only a few examples of the limitless frustrations that can come from developing strong personal relationships within your team.

Sadly, there are many times when abuse takes place in these relationships when it is not intended at all. This happens when reactions are based on the perception of the relationship that we have learned and developed from our own family members and other personal relationships. People who are abused are more guarded, or sometimes can be more attacking of others. Sometimes people who come from different backgrounds and cultures open up, and are much more easily offended by others. The differences in personal upbringing throughout your team makes personal relationships difficult. The point being, the more personal a relationship in your team is, despite the initial feel of control, ultimately is something the leader has even less control over than they perceive.

This is also not to mention the increased likelihood that being overly familiar with someone, like a leader, can lead members of your team to actually take your guidance and direction for granted. It is similar to family members who have distinguished professionals among their siblings, who would never ask them for advice on their specialty. Not because they are not qualified in any way, but because they are their little brother, they are familiar with them, and no matter how respected they are in the professional world, they can't see past the time they got candy stuck up their nose, or got a black eye from walking into a glass door. Being too familiar with some people can actually be detrimental to the influence that one party can have on another.

On the other end of the spectrum, strictly professional relationships are not appealing to very many people in this industry, either. This is because as you network, you are naturally attracted to people most like you. You find and develop friendships. Additionally, there are people who will join your team, not to have a professional relationship with people, but for the social aspect of being a part of your team. Many people need to feel more connected to something other than their everyday "professional" life.

So what are we to do?

This is where we as leaders find ourselves in a fickle bind. We can't have personal relationships with everyone without finding ourselves emotionally overwhelmed and ultimately ineffective, and we can't be effective if we only have professional relationships with our team because no one wants to join another "job."

As a leader, the mastery of the personal-professional relationship is important. This is done by finding ways to be involved in their lives, to listen to them, encourage them personally, while still maintaining important boundaries with them. Learn about them, praise them, be a small part of their lives. This is a personal must. People need to know that you care as a leader and you need to be genuine about it. But as a leader, make sure that you are comfortable that it is not a two-way street; they do not need to care about you. Realizing that this is a one way street, and that what you get in return is seeing them succeed and, in turn, giving you greater success, can be a foundation to developing this personal-professional relationship. You engage with them personally, caring about them and seeking their good. In turn, they will develop a love for you as a leader, because they know that you will care for them. But you will restrict yourself from opening your personal door to them. You will be entirely professional on your end with what you share about your life, your family, and your personal life. You will give to them personally, and not expect, encourage, or in some instances, even allow them to reciprocate that personal relationship.

As humans, we play in what sociologists call the "Zone of Intimacy." This is the law in which relationships are developed. It says that when someone shares something with someone else of a personal nature, it is naturally reciprocated in some fashion with an equally intimate comment or action – thus developing the relationship through shared personal information. This exchange can take days or years to happen, but it happens. As a leader, knowing how this works is knowing where your limitations are in developing your relationships. You will ask, listen, and let them share – taking steps toward you. You will respond and encourage, and let them develop into better people. But you will restrict your own steps towards them. You will be professional in how you respond, not over-sharing about your personal life, your marriage, or personal finances. You will not place on your team expectations for them to live up to your relationship.

What you will find, is that this rule is not the only way people develop relationships but it is most natural way. People will still move closer to you in this zone - even without you sharing personal information but merely by acknowledging their personal information and help them develop a love, not for your life, but for your ear, encouragement, and your direction.

## What You Do or Don't Do

One of the simplest lessons in leadership within Network Marketing is that what you do or what you don't do duplicates. This is the same rule that is found in many parenting books. What you do every day, or what is seen being done by others, is what other people will consider doing themselves. The flip side to this coin is that what you don't do, and are seen not doing also duplicates.

Remember those sad drug commercials decades ago about the parent who found drugs in their son's room? When the parent confronted the son, his reply was "I learned it from watching you." It was a somewhat funny scene, even then, but the principle is true in many ways of life.

Much of your team don't know what they should be doing, or what they shouldn't be doing. The options for them to follow, act upon, or do in life come not from what is really available as an option, but what they see as being present to them as an option. This means that if they never see someone do an action, it will never enter into their minds that the action can, should, or even could be taken. That action is never placed on the menu of things that they could possibly do. So the first thing to realize is that if your team doesn't see you doing something, they themselves will never even consider it an option of something for them do. If you want something done in your team, then you need to make sure you are doing it. You also need to make sure that others are seeing, hearing, and learning from you doing it.

The other side of the coin is that even if they know something is an option, but you are not doing it, that activity will duplicate as well. If you don't do something, you need to expect that they will not do the action either.

Once you realize that you need to place the correct actions on the menu for them to choose from, what you choose yourself will be the most influential actions in what others will try to do.

This small lesson exhausts or condemns even the most well-meaning of leaders in the industry. There are times when a leader is comfortable with a single action in their business that works for them, or maybe even they are at a point in their career that they choose to take the road less successful out of comfort. Even though this activity would not be a great success for their team, they stick to it themselves, and then wonder why their team is not successful. Meanwhile, their team tries hard to succeed but ultimately is doing an activity that doesn't yield much success. This happens only because that is what they see their leader doing.

This was seen a few years ago with one leader I worked closely with. This leader had built their business the hard way – through expo center booths. This is not the easiest way to build a business - and even harder to teach duplication with - but this was something that they were comfortable with. Even with the messaging of the company being focused on home parties, their team could not seem to get past the idea of doing expensive and relatively unsuccessful expos. This was solely based on the impression that was left by the leader. Even the leader knew that it wasn't the best way to build a successful team, and she would encourage others to take another path – but her actions were what seemed to influence her team much more than any words or training she gave could.

Realizing this will help you understand the behavior of your team, and the team members of others.

The actions you choose to take as a leader within your organization, and the actions you personally take to build your own team, are the same actions that are more likely to be duplicated throughout your team. We see this time and time again. If a leader enrolls on the highest starter package available, it is more likely to see people in their team also sign up with the same option. If the leader is on every company phone call, they always have a higher count on the call within their own team. If a leader is regularly enrolling, attending corporate events or conventions, ordering large quantities of product, pounding the pavement, and working hard – that activity is more likely to be seen within their organization. What you do within your organization is what you will see your organization do more of.

In addition to that, what you don't do also duplicates within your team. Leaders who don't get on calls, don't order product, don't take it seriously, or do not engage in high levels within the company will see that same activity – or lack of activity - take place within their team.

This is a rule in this industry that leaves us with a critical realization: Engage wholeheartedly, and do the things that you want others to do.

## Being The Top 5% - Easier Than You Think

This is going to sound almost too simple to even take a complete section, but it is one of the concepts in leadership that needs to be said to anyone who wishes to accomplish any of their leadership goals.

The SIMPLE CONCEPT: If you want to be in the top 5% of Network Marketing in recruiting, in earnings, and in momentum, then you only need to do more than the other 95% of network marketers.

THE SIMPLE SECRET: Doing more than 95% of people in Network Marketing is easier than you think because 95% of people don't do much at all!

If you want to be in the top 5%, you only need to dedicate yourself to doing more than those who don't do much at all. Our lives are based upon trying to do the least amount of work for the most amount of money, and within Network Marketing we find ourselves in an environment where a lot of people are not doing much at all, if anything. In fact, this environment leads many people to justify their lack of activity because of everyone else's lack of activity. When in reality, their lack of activity only lowers the bar of leadership and accomplishment for the rest of us.

Look around and see what everyone else is doing, and then do more – it is as simple as that! Make more phone calls, have more parties, and do more to build your business. It really isn't that hard once you realize how little everyone else is doing. In sum, it may only be a means of trying more often to build your business than the rest of everyone else.

Those people who are used to doing more in life find that in this industry, it is easy to rise to the top because most people don't do much at all. You want to make more than the guy next to you – that is easy, just do more than he does (which isn't much). That is the simple rule of reaching the top 5%.

Now that same rule applies to those within the 5%, only now you are playing with people who really know how to do more! But you can still compete. You can continue to do more and build yourself up through those ranks.

Realize that it is easier than you think it is to be in the top 5%; in fact more people self-eliminate themselves based on their assumptions that they can't do it, or that it is too much work. As a result, they hesitated in doing anything at all and contribute to the reality that 95% can be beat by just putting forth a little consistent effort.

# Pace Someone Faster (Marathon Part 1)

Now that you have learned the secret to getting in the top 5% of any company in this industry, let's talk about getting higher than that – the top 1-2%.

To get to the top 5% you only needed to move faster, or do more in your day to day activities than most people – which isn't difficult to do. It just takes "doing" to accomplish that. Yet, in this process of "doing" anything to reach some success, we learn through trial and error what works for us and what doesn't work for us. We may not know this, but these lessons are out there for us to pick up on if we are ready to notice them.

Then something happens in a growing leader's organization around the time they start growing past the 5% mark and beyond to larger leadership levels. They start to look around at what other people are doing in their organization, and question their own actions in building their business. Rather than rely on the activities that got them to their current success to take them to the next level, they start looking for new and unique ways to build their business that they may be discovering through the growing (yet still smaller) members of their team.

This naturally seems like a positive business decision – to be open to new ideas and strategies; but it is focused on the wrong side of the race.

If we were to pretend that your leadership experience is like a long race, maybe a marathon, or other feat of endurance, what these leaders are doing is detrimental to their immediate and long term future success. In essence, what each leader is doing is, instead of looking forward and staying consistent – they are looking backwards at the team they are leading, and watching how they are running. They are looking at the people behind them, who are slower than they are, and trying to pace with or copy them. This is done in fear that someone behind them will discover some trick and pass them by without warning.

Why would a leader, who has already generated some type of success in an organization look to those who have less success, are moving slower than they are, and attempt to mimic their activity in hopes that they would somehow stumble upon something that they could use?

In reality, what each leader in this feat of endurance needs to do is not look back at their team for new ideas, or techniques to build. They need to stay consistent with the activity they already know generates them success. They need to look ahead and consider mimicking those who have greater success. In a race like a marathon, or a feat of endurance like leadership, if you want to improve, you try and keep pace with someone faster or more successful than you. A leader doesn't look back in fear or desperation, a leader looks forward to learn more successful actions and refine their skills by observing those who are more successful.

Respect your team, and support them in the success that they have and can generate with their path. But remember, it is personally important that you seek to look ahead, mimic those more successful than you – and avoid trying to mimic those members of your team who are less successful.

# Consistency (Marathon Part 2)

To continue the marathon theme – leadership and building your business is more like a marathon than most people realize. If you are anything like me, you challenge the notion that a marathon (running or walking 26.2 miles) should be classified as a "race." This is because the term "race" denotes that there is a winner, because someone moved faster than everyone else. This inherently leads us to the idea of there being "losers" in the marathon – but this is not true.

If we are honest with ourselves, we can honestly say that a marathon is not a race, because no ONE person really WINS the marathon. I believe that a marathon WINNER (singular) is a myth. I have never personally met anyone who WINS a marathon. I think the idea that someone actually crosses the finish line in only a few hours is somehow a conspiracy by someone somewhere for some devious purpose – which I don't understand.

When you run a marathon, you don't get a medal for being the first across the finish line. You get the medal for crossing the finish line. A marathon is not a "race" to see who is faster, but is a feat of personal endurance to see who can continue on the path for an extended period of time (26.2 miles). In fact, it is not even a complicated feat of endurance, but maybe even more challenging is the feat of consistency in taking the most simple action – one step in front of the other – over and over and over again. It is not to see who can go the fastest, look the prettiest doing it, or even who can come up with the most unique way to move on the course. It is all about whether you can take the simple action of taking a single step, for an extended period of time.

This is leadership and the key to building your business. It is not a race to see who can get to the highest rank the fastest, or even faster than anyone else. It is a feat of personal endurance. Endurance defined by your ability to take the same simple actions over and over again for an extended period of time (longer than others can) – and whether you can remain consistent in that simple behavior. It is about whether you can learn what works for you, and whether you can continue that action and behavior through hell or high-water.

In a marathon, the same action that takes you through your first mile is the same action that takes you through your twenty-fifth mile. In leadership, often times the same simple behaviors that get you through your first ranks are the same simple behaviors that will and should carry you through your last ranks.

In a marathon, when you finish the final mile you are thrilled that your crossed it – whether you were the third one over the line or the three hundredth participate over the line. In leadership, you won't care whether it took you three months, three years, or thirty years when that check comes – it will be worth it, and it will be a life changing experience. Focus less on speed, and more on consistent endurance on the simple steps ahead of you.

## Avoid Boredom (Marathon Part 3)

Now in this marathon that we call leadership, we need to discuss a very real threat to your business. It a something that often goes unnoticed, but has the potential to stall your business faster than anything else.

When I was training for my first marathon, I discovered a number of things about myself – and about you!

I discovered that if I put my mind to something, I could do amazing things. When I started training, I learned that as long as I remained consistent, and really wanted something, I could progress and grow rather quickly. I found that I could add distance and improve my time on my long runs weekly.

After a week of standard training, I would dedicate a number of hours each Saturday to a long run. Each week I would try and add miles to my long run – and each week I was successful. This was until I hit mile eleven in my training.

The first time I did eleven miles, I thought I was going to die. I had to stop and call my wife to come and pick me up. I was exhausted and worn out for the rest of the weekend. The next week on my long run, I found I still could not pass eleven miles, and I hobbled back to the house. The third week was the same, and for the next few weeks I continued to hit a wall at the eleven mile mark. By about the fifth or sixth week at eleven miles, I noticed something. Although I couldn't go any further, it was getting easier and easier to do that eleven mile run. Around week five, I did my run, then came home, played soccer with the kids at the park and then did a family activity that evening. This was a far cry from the first week where I barely got off the couch.

It was at the end of this particular Saturday that I realized something odd. My wife (as usual) made the obvious comment that put everything in place. I started to express to her that I was perplexed by the fact that I really couldn't go any further than eleven miles, and yet I still obviously had energy the rest of the day. When I commented on this puzzle, she looked at me and simply said, "You get bored." It hit me like a ton of bricks – she was right! As slow as I am, after two and a half hours of running, I was getting bored. I wasn't hitting a wall of physical capability I was hitting a mental wall. My brain couldn't stay entertained and mentally engaged in the process.

This happens in our lives anytime we try anything that requires endurance – particularly leadership and building our businesses. This is one of the most dangerous threats because it can so easily go unnoticed, and yet can affect everything so quickly.

As we first start to build our business, it is new and exciting and it's easy for us to remain entertained. Eventually as leaders we learn what works and we start getting into a pattern of what to do, as we start to refine our skills. Then at some point in our feat of endurance, we hit mile eleven. Whether we recognize it consciously or not – we get bored. We start to look around at what everyone else is doing, what everyone else is talking about, and we start looking for other things to keep us entertained.

The threat here is that as we start looking for new things, we start to neglect the easy, simple, and proven things that grow our business. There is not one leader in this industry that is immune to boredom. Everyone will suffer from it eventually, and the true judge of whether they finish the race is whether they succumb to it or suffer through it.

When a leader succumbs to it, they start to look at other activities, and try new things. They try these things and replace those that have worked in the past for them. They change their behavior, and their results change (usually not positively). They find that they are still working hard, and expending a lot of energy doing so (more than before), but that they are not gaining any additional success or even maintaining the success they had before. They start to get discouraged and they lose sight of what actually worked. This is where leaders start to get lost, and begin to question why their business has stalled or plateaued (this is where the activity in *Manage your "Arrival"* and *"Why Is My Business Stalled?"* is important). If this isn't fixed, a leader may never fully acknowledge what changed, and their business can be stalled forever.

When a leader makes the decision to suffer through it, they look down at their feet and focus on the simple steps that keep them moving forward toward their goal. They sometimes need to block out their surroundings, their environment, and even advice from their team, and work on staying steady on the path that they already know is working for them. They learn to be satisfied with the pace they are running, knowing that they are still moving towards the goal. As long as they are growing, they are satisfied. They realize that any deviation from this path is a risk to their business and their future.

As a leader, it is important to acknowledge boredom, avoid it if you can, and if you can't, stay consistent and power through it like a real leader does.

# Know When to Look Up and When to Look Down (Marathon Part 4)

Developing a proper leadership perspective isn't only about how you think about yourself and leadership, but how you behave with yourself and with your team. It isn't just about thought. It is also about action.

To reach the end result of having an appropriate leadership perspective, you must develop a leadership action. These actions then need to be consistently and steadily repeated over an extended period of time.

To do this, you need to learn enough about yourself, to allow you to know when to look up and when to look down. Let me explain:

There are important times in our lives when we need to be able to see the big picture. We need to see the full potential, of what we know or hope we can accomplish. We need to see that big check, that beautiful dream board with the black sports car or the larger house, or maybe even that dream vacation. We need to see those goals and potential accomplishments, and they should be motivating to us. They should get us started on our path and help us begin fulfilling our true potential. Seeing that 26.2 mile course, that finish line, that medal, and the pride of saying you've finished a marathon should be something that should get you out on that course. This is what is called looking up, and taking in the big picture. Looking up at the big picture can - and should be - very motivating to begin with.

But there comes a time in every feat of endurance, where for any number of potential reasons, looking up can not only be painful, but actually discouraging. When you hit mile eleven in your marathon, or your business, looking up and seeing that you are not even halfway done can demolish your confidence in your ability, and challenge your ability to continue. Sometimes looking up at the big picture hurts much more than it helps.

When those moments come, the most important thing for you to do is to look down. In running, this means looking down at your feet, ignoring the finish line, the medal, and the final goal. Just focus on the simple steps ahead of you. Focusing on just putting one foot in front of the other. Be humble enough in your business and honest enough with yourself to know when the big picture is too much for you to look at. Then be courageous enough to put your head down, ignore it, and focus only on the small simple steps that are ahead of you. Keep moving. Keep going. Keep growing.

The secret within this tip is that whether you keep your head up or you keep looking down, the same simple actions, the same steps, will carry you to the same finish line. There is no shame in changing your perspective from the grand to the simple in order to survive – there is only shame in failure because you gave up prematurely.

# No Excuses

As a leader within the organization, understanding and training your team that there are no excuses can be an important moment within your development.

We do not always intend to do so, but we are regularly looking for excuses not to do things. The interesting thing is, when we view something as optional in our lives (like building a home-based-business), anything can be an excuse not to do that optional activity.

For instance, we can consider the important steps to take our business to the next level. We can list them out and realize exactly what we need to do every day to make our dreams a success. At that point, the only thing left to do is to do them.

Then we wake up one morning, with the intention of starting in on those activities. We look out the window and discover that the weather is terrible. It could be raining outside, it may be snowing at times, and maybe there are literally cats and dogs falling from the sky. We then justify in ourselves that it is a terrible day to do those activities, and we are fully comfortable and justified to postponing our actions until the next day. We think we have a good excuse to do so.

The interesting thing about human behavior is what happens the next day. We wake up that morning, and look out the window and the storm has passed. Not only has it passed, but it is one of the most beautiful days we have ever seen. The sun is out, the humidity is right, and the temperature is projected to be a perfect 72 degrees all day. We realize that the day is too good to miss, and we justify postponing whatever activities we were planning that day so we can go and enjoy the day.

There is always a reason not to work. There will always be a way to justify why we cannot or should not do what is planned or necessary to grow our business. It may be too good of a day - or too terrible of a day – the reality is, there will always be "days" to say, "not today." True leadership is realizing that regardless of circumstances, you will remain consistent in your commitment to yourself, your family, your team, and your business. You will not allow yourself to create excuses. You will not let the weather, your environment, or your circumstances, stop you from doing the small things that you know you need to do to keep your business going, growing, and thriving.

There will always be a reason not to do what you know you need to, but you need to be the one who decides that none of that matters.

There will be times when there are good reasons to genuinely take a break from your daily dedication to your business. There are real tragedies in everyone's life, and real heartache. In those times, realize it is those moments that you work so hard for – so that you can stop and take stock of what is truly important. Be cautious, never let anything short of those truly valid reasons become an excuse to postpone or delay an activity that you know full well can - and should - be done now.

No excuses. There is no excuse to not do your daily activities for your business.

# Are You Serving?

Nearly every extremely successful leader will tell you, "My business changed when I stopped thinking about what others can do for me, and started thinking about what my business and I can do for them."

This statement is the foundation of many successful businesses. When a leader changes their perspective from inward, to outward, people respond differently and their business goes through the roof. Another related comment that I hear often is, "When I make sure that others are taken care of, I find all my needs are taken care of as well."

The question that each leader, or aspiring leader should ask themselves is, "Are you serving others with your business?"

Asking yourself how your business opportunity, product, or leadership can help someone else will not only make your job easier and your team respond better to you, you will find it much more fulfilling emotionally, spiritually, and financially. When you think of others first, you will discover something remarkable about Network Marketing that is difficult to put into words, but can often only be experienced.

RYAN DALEY

# Part 5
# Leadership Duplication

# Duplication

The difference between finding success on the sweat of your own work (which is required at all levels of leadership), and finding exponential success through the power of leveraging other's is significant. It is the difference between finding full-time earnings that give you and your family the freedom you want to enjoy your lives, and finding excessive earnings with true unlimited potential that can give you the stability of a bank account with enough money that you honestly wouldn't know what to do with.

This difference is realized through the power of duplication. Duplication is the means by which you train others to work and behave in a particular way to build success for themselves. Within the power of Network Marketing, the potential for you to succeed as they build success also grows. In this discussion, the leader needs to realize the power of duplication (duplicating their efforts through multiple people) as well realize the two separate forms of duplication – each form requiring a different level of attention.

It should be assumed from previous chapters and sections that the potential and power of duplication within Network Marketing is understood. The difference between the two categories of duplication is critical for the leader to fine tune their skills, actions, and in turn, their success.

True leadership is not about developing followers. It is about developing other leaders.

The next two sections will help us define and apply these two forms of duplication.

## Maximizing Two Different Duplications

When most people talk about duplication in Network Marketing they are generally referring to Active Duplication; although at times they may mistakenly discuss it in conjunction with the other form of duplication. Active Duplication refers to the type of activity that takes place within an organization. This encompasses the trained skills and technics of building the business which are perpetuated throughout a team. This form of duplication is needed in every organization to build a team.

Active Duplication is what you do, or attempt to do, when you teach new members of your team how you built your organization, and, how they can build their organization. This type of duplication will be adhered to in various degrees which, despite potential frustrations, is expected. It is important to note that and any leader will tell you that any level of duplication is accepted (a little duplication is better than no duplication). With this form of duplication, everything helps.

This form of duplication is also seen when you create realistic goals within your organization for them to reach on an organizational or individual level. This is where instead of telling someone to shoot for the highest levels of the compensation plan, you are teaching them small steps towards achieving certain goals. Some of these skills may include making a list of potential customers or distributors, attempting to enroll two people in their first thirty days (and then attempting to have them train their team to do the same), or turning around and doing some basic activity that will drive their organization. Active Duplication in its simplest form is when a leader tries to teach their team how to grow their business in simple steps that if everyone repeated, would build a remarkable organization (e.g. they get two people, and help them get two people, and so on and so forth). This form of duplication is critical, a must for any team, and is what most people think of when it comes to duplication.

The second form of duplication is also important, but it is just as important not to confuse the two. This form of duplication is Leadership Duplication.

It is a hard truth, but not everyone in your team is a leader, going to be a leader, or even wants to be a leader. Leadership Duplication is not for everyone on your team; it may not even be for many of those who say they want it. A good time within Network Marketing will teach any leader that there is a difference between what people say they are willing to do, or wish to be, and what they will really do or really become.

If you want to have success within Network Marketing, you are required to spend your days teaching and training your entire team the skills and concepts that will yield Active Duplication, while Leadership Duplication is really only for those who can handle it. When a leader doesn't understand the difference and attempts to group these two concepts together, they often disenfranchise those members of their team who are willing and capable of some form of duplication but are unwilling to develop the leadership qualities needed. As a leader, not knowing the difference can yield undeserved frustration as a result. You may stop working with some team members because they are not listening to your feedback when in reality, they are just not listening to those messages which are beyond their capacity to understand in their current position. Leadership is ultimately a choice, and no amount of training can change someone's mind – it becomes something they choose to develop within themselves, not something you can force upon them. Knowing the difference between the two types of duplication is critical to fine tuning your activity and magnifying your success.

You will, and should, teach EVERYONE the simple program and steps it takes to develop their business step-by-step (Active Duplication), but you should only attempt to teach LEADERS developmental skills on how to be the best leaders they can be (Leadership Duplication). Otherwise, everyone else gets overwhelmed with leadership skills they do not currently have the capability to understand – and the masses are no longer doing even the simple steps that you need to duplicate in order to grow your business.

Leadership Duplication is about teaching the principles in this book; not to create a different type of activity, but to create a different caliber of person. It is about creating and changing someone's nature into a leader, and focusing on the development of the person as a whole – which as a consequence, changes their behavior.

As you build your team, 98% will need to understand the notion of duplication and will need to be trained on those simple skills of Active Duplication. Only 2% of your team will be ready and capable of learning and applying Leadership Duplication. If you only have the Active Duplication from 98%, you will find great success within your organization and this should be a worthy goal. As you teach those skills, you will begin to see the 2% rise to the top naturally. When you are able to develop Leadership Duplication within that 2%, your great success becomes legendary – and you will find yourself on top of an indestructible organization.

# Master Your Message

To teach Leadership Duplication, you must first be a true leader yourself. It sounds like too simple and basic a concept to mention, but in reality it is the most important concept needed in order to teach leadership. You must be the master of your message. You must understand everything that you are teaching. You must know it, because you have lived it. You must try everything you attempt to teach, rather than attempt only to teach concepts and philosophies. Those who have experienced the results will always be greater teachers than those who have not.

You cannot teach something that you do not know yourself, or that you have an intimate knowledge of.

When working with growing leaders in various organizations, it is always a temptation for them to attempt to build leadership within their organization prematurely. This is because they attempt to elevate others to higher levels than they are at themselves. This fundamentally does not work. You cannot lift someone to higher ground than you yourself are on – and if you could, you wouldn't want to.

What does work is studying, applying, and developing yourself as a leader. Mastering the skills in this book, as well as in any other materials that you can get your hands on will help in that process. Learn the difference between philosophy and application. Learn what works and what doesn't, and most importantly why it works, and why it doesn't. This will help you become credible, and you will be able to give unique insights to members of your team from your own experiences that will help them apply the concepts you share. A leader cannot teach duplication, if they have never learned what it means to apply it themselves.

# Repetition Is the Law of Learning

As you train your team, whether you are teaching Active Duplication principles or leadership concepts, do not be tempted to change your message. Repetition is the law of learning. Teach principles that you are passionate about and that you know to work again and again. Do it until you do it in your sleep – and then keep doing it.

There is a temptation for leaders at every level to change their presentations and messaging often. They do this because they think to themselves that they have trained on the topic already. They think that people have already heard it and that they would be bored. What they may also be thinking is that they have heard it and taught it already and they are tired of the message. This temptation often generates a desire to "find something new" and aspiring leaders start to teach and focus on less effective things in an effort to avoid being "boring." This is usually a mistake and oversight.

Successful leaders must learn a few things.

First, in order to achieve real duplication in any principle, their team must actually hear the idea or concept that they want applied. To do this, the message must be shared. After they share the message, when they get a chance to share it again, they do so - again and again. They realize that there are people in the room, on the call, or on the webinar that have never heard that message before. There are those who are new to their team and those who may have been trained on the topic thirty times; there may be thirty people who haven't heard the message yet. They also know that even those who have heard the message may not have actually heard or fully understood the message – and they need to hear the repetition to fully understand it or learn it. And finally, even those who have heard and understood it more than likely haven't fully applied it, and therefore need to be reminded about it again in order to be inspired about how they might be able to apply it in their business.

For these leaders, repetition is not only the law of learning, it is really the only law of growing.

They know that hearing a message once is never enough to actually inspire people to apply it.

Marketers know this truth in very powerful ways. They know that it takes you seven times to see a brand before you will even acknowledge that the brand exists. It will also take you seven times to see a billboard on the road before you actually read what it says. This is what experts call the "rule of seven." The same applies to any other concept when a message is trying to be relayed. A leader will need to teach a concept to someone seven times before an individual can begin to feel confident in applying it – let alone mastering it.

Repeat your message regardless of how many times you have done it already. You might have heard it a million times, but there may be a million people hearing it only for the first time. Don't change your message out of your own boredom, you will only risk the growth of your team.

# The Last Temptation of the Pleaser

In every company or organization that I have every worked with, there has been always a consistent philosophy that I consider to be the worst sin of leadership. That is gifting, rewarding, or placing people or enrollments under other people prematurely.

As some people try to be leaders without having the basic skills to help inspire others to grow and take action themselves, some of these "want to be leaders" seek to please their team by helping them build a structure. So rather than empowering and encouraging them to go and build their own team, these leaders go ahead and try and do it for them. They meet a friend, and tell them "I'll put some people under you" to "help them out."

Sometimes this is a recruiting technique, and sometimes this is just to be friendly and supporting. Either way, this can cause some significant complications.

First, this creates an entitled culture within your organization. Rather than teaching your team how to fish, you are just handing fish to them. With this, you haven't actually helped them develop anything; you have just given them something that they learn to expect in the future. When they find that this industry is a little harder than they may have expected, rather than dig in and work harder, they will look to you and wonder where the next handout is. Why would they work so hard for that second enrollment, when the first enrollment was just handed to them?

Second, this creates jealousy within the organization. As people talk, and pride is shared, it eventually gets around that the leader gave an enrollment to someone else. Questions start arising, and discouragement sets in as the team wonders why that was done in one organization and not in another. Fractions then begin within the team.

Third, this puts a greater threat with the newly enrolled member than is usually expected. As they are placed under someone who may not be a leader themselves, the new member is somewhat subject to someone else's lack of experience. Where their new and inexperienced upline goes (usually not in a positive direction), so will the new member. In addition to the potential of future complications with the new member, there are current complications as they develop the feeling of being expendable. When a leader works to sign someone up and then assigns them to someone not as experienced, it can give the new member a feeling that maybe there wasn't a lot of confidence in them; enough so, that they were given to someone else. They may begin to feel like pawns in a game.

Needless to say, regardless of the intentions of these well-meaning leaders to support people – most of the results of this temptation are not positive.

This is not entirely to say that a leader doesn't place people in the organization over time. It is to say that they do not place new members in the organization as a means to please someone else, build a struggling organization, or try and structure some support. True leaders will eventually place individuals, but they will only place with those members of their team who are also true leaders, who have lasted the test of time, and those who can genuinely give the support that a new member would like and need.

## Share, Share, Share

There is a small germ that seems to take some distributors in this industry and make them sick. It is what I call the secret germ. This is where a leader, or a hopeful leader, learns something in their business that really works, and it works well. As a result, they think they have stumbled upon some secret, and maybe they have. The last thing they want to do is share this discovery with their team.

They think that if they share this discovery with their team, somehow this secret will be less valuable to them. This germ needs to be killed!

Share what you learn about your business with your team. Only when you teach and train your team what works can you expect them to have the success that you have. Only when they have the success that you have, can you reap the rewards that Network Marketing promises you. Your team has to succeed in order for you to really succeed. Share your knowledge, your secrets, and your growth with them. You may be surprised how much they can help make those secrets you discover even more effective.

Sometimes the lack of sharing experience with a team is not intentional. It is not always as a result of some secret discovery. Sometimes it is a lack of appreciation or self-confidence that you really do know what works. Each person with a team under them needs to have the confidence to know that something they did worked on some level. Sharing everything that you know has worked with your team, even when you acknowledge that you might not know everything, can be extremely impactful to the growth of your team.

Only when you share your knowledge can you duplicate your success – there is no way around it. Share, share, share!

# Part Six
# Leadership Finances

# Finances of a Leader

A commonly overlooked virtue of a leader is financial responsibility. Even the most successful "leaders" in the industry, who are making hundreds of thousands to millions of dollars a year, do not have this virtue, and as a result, are unable to actually experience the freedom that they have earned and qualified for. Hundreds of people have experienced success in this industry without actually learning how to enjoy it. This is primarily because they have never developed the discipline needed to create a foundation of security within any level of income.

I have worked with hundreds of distributors who have made anywhere from $1,000 extra a month to $1,000,000 a year and still have financial problems. Financial leadership is a critical skill to develop as a leader, because the development of this needed discipline will spread over into every other area of leadership. This will also allow you to, in turn, teach and train others the needed discipline, and as a result, create stronger and more secure teams.

When a leader or a team member has not developed the financial leadership necessary to be secure and experience true freedom from their effort, they find themselves becoming a slave to the income. They find that they are forced to fight for that income, and they actually become much less stable in the development of their teams. When those ebbs come in, panic may set in, behavior changes that month, and suddenly momentum changes.

As a leader, you not only need to develop this security for you and your family, you will need to be an example of this security for your team as you try and duplicate this training among them.

Do not wait to develop this financial discipline. Develop these qualities now, or early when your check is low, as this will define how effectively you can apply these principles.

When I teach this principle, I am reminded of my first few years of marriage. In my early twenties, we were both young with two young children. I was in school, and working full time making slightly more than minimum wage. Finances were difficult to say the least, but we had a few financial goals. One of those goals was to be able to allow my wife to stay at home with the children and be a full time mom (this was her decision more than it was mine). At that point, we made the decision to find a way to have the financial disciple then, when we had virtually no money. We committed to make it work, sacrifice what we needed, and we figured that if we could make it work on that low of an income, we could make it work on any level of income. This was one of the greatest decisions we have ever made. We made it work, and it was true. Living off of that low income, while still fulfilling our commitments, proved that at any time we could make it happen.

I knew that as our income expanded, our behavior would expand with it. This is also a true concept. Humans are much like sharks - we will grow in proportion to the tank we are in. Our spending will naturally grow into the income that we are earning. This means that if we don't manage our financial activity from the onset, when our income increases, our behavior will conform within those habits to absorb that increase. As leaders, we must set our finances in order now, so that as they increase, will naturally increase into more stability, rather than less stability.

Within this section you will find a recommendation for handling your finances in relation to your business. You should note that this in only in relation to your home-based business and you are encouraged to make any adjustment necessary. Following this basic foundation for the revenue generated in your business will be a benefit to you and will give you a foundation to learn to experience a degree of freedom at any level of success.

It should be noted that these concepts are only suggestions, and depending upon the specifics of your business, you should feel comfortable to make any necessary adjustments. What is important is not the exact ratio of each section that you adhere to, but that you make room for the concepts in each section. Each business, home, family, and financial needs are different, but as you make room in your budget for each section as you and your family dictate, you will find a security that only comes from the discipline of managing your funds wisely.

It is also encouraged as a leader that you learn more about your personal finances outside of your business. Track your expenses to make sure you get every benefit you possibly can from having your home-based business.

NOTE: This is the last section of leadership because, although the concept of financial discipline is a critical one for each leader, this is the section where the specific application of that development will vary from person to person. These sections are not as universally applicable as the other sections.

## Retail Sales – The Foundation for Stability

In selecting a Network Marketing company, many leaders and distributors overlook the importance of Retail Sales. For many, a retail program is only a by-product of the opportunity. For those who are serious about managing their finances in their home based business, the effectiveness of the retail program is critical to their success.

A leader can be finically successful without a strong retail program; however, it becomes significantly easier to become profitable and to create a financial foundation for success the stronger the retail program is.

This is because your retail profit and sale, become the foundation for your financial success. As you work towards generating retail sales, and in turn, retail profit, you should find yourself naturally building an organization of distributors and your residual check.

Initially, your first goal is to have your retail profit and earnings cover the cost of doing your business. As you progress through the development of your business, the cost of doing business changes its definition. As you start your business in a part-time setting, your cost of doing business will be the cost of doing that business while you are working it. This might include gas for meetings, advertising, inventory and tool purchases, and other training skills.

As your skills increase and you become more effective at recruiting and retail sales, your secondary goal is for your cost of doing business to include your living expenses. This would include your mortgage, car payment, and other monthly bills. Having a business opportunity that can facilitate this strong of a retail program gives the leader a significant advantage in their finances over another. At this stage you can then justify to yourself your ability to "go full-time" into the business.

With this concept, your residual team check comes more as a

bonus than as a sustaining necessity. Also, as you are committed to this concept, you will find yourself continuing to work through phases where others would stop. You will work harder for your retail profit knowing that your bills rely upon it, and you will not let your day to day lifestyle be defined by others (the success of your team). As you work more diligently while other rest, you will find the work ethic of your team increase, your team grow more stable, and your will continue to fill you team and grow as others shrink. This activity is strongly tied to the concept of when you have "arrived" which was discussed in an earlier chapter.

In sum, your retail profit should be what you use to pay for your inventory, your personal product, and your basic business expenses. Eventually, this should grow to cover basic living expenses as you decide to go full-time. The rest of your residual earnings (your commission check) should be allocated to other purposes. This basic concept of retail profit gives the distributor a unique foundational financial advantage, which those who do not have or carry a strong retail market with their product will not experience.

The rest of the sections within this part will deal with effective ways to handle and deal with your residual or commission check from month-to-month or week-to-week to develop a secure foundation. Of course, I recommend speaking with your accountant and an official tax accountant to determine what the best course is for you.

## "The Tax Man" Account – 30%

There is no getting around it. You are going to have to pay taxes on your earnings. There are some important things that you can do to minimize what you pay, but you will still need to pay something.

With this in mind, it is recommended that you create an account that is set apart from the rest of your accounts, and that you immediately deposit 30% of your earnings into. This is a fairly safe number that will allow you to be prepared to pay the government when the time comes every year and to make sure that there are no surprises. One of the most devastating things you can do is to be unprepared for taxes, having already spent what you will eventually owe. It can pull your attention away from your business around tax time and place a sense of unnecessary urgency to generate more money in order to pay the tax bill every April. The suggested 30% will not only help you be prepared for taxes, but it will create a peace of mind and a greater sense of security at tax time; making that painful time less burdensome on your building activity, and on your team.

To some 30% will seem like a good guess, and to others it may seem somewhat excessive - and it hopefully is. I am not suggesting that you should be paying 30% to the government; I am saying that you should be prepared to. Outside of preparing, you should do everything in your power to pay the least amount of taxes that you are responsible for. This will require that you treat your business as a business. This requires that you keep track of your mileage and travel expenses; that you keep every receipt that may potentially apply; and that you keep an eye on how much of your cell phone, your house, and other resources you are using for your business. It is highly recommended that you not only attempt to keep track of these things on your own, but that you use one of the many tax and expense tracker programs for home based businesses. These will not only help you keep track and minimize tax liability legally, but it can also provide critical education towards helping you maximize your spending in your business to get the most tax benefit and the most bang for every buck. Eventually, you may want to hire an accountant, but for many that might be seen as an unnecessary expense, especially in the beginning.

As the goal of all this is to minimize your tax liability so that you might actually pay less taxes, you might think that you can be "smart" and put less away for taxes. That is not recommended. Plan for the 30%, then work every angle you can to minimize your liability according to your tax responsibility. Then when you come to that tax season every year, do what you can to complete your taxes as early as possible. This will be exciting because you will see every penny that you planned to pay, that you actually didn't pay, as a bonus. If, or when you find yourself paying less than you saved for the year – take that as a bonus. Allocate those extra funds immediately into an account towards your short or long term goals, or take that extra money and spend it on yourself. This is where you get to have this bonus because you were smart with your taxes!

Put 30% of your residual income every check within a tax account. After taxes are filed, every dollar that is not paid but was saved, goes to you to spend as you see fit (splurge on yourself, or put it towards one of your long term or short term goals).

## A Generous Giver is a Generous Receiver – 10%

Many of the most successful people in the world are extremely giving. It is often a misunderstanding in the world to think that they were generous because they had so much to give; when the reality is, they often became successful because the characteristic of generosity is one which supports success.

It is recommended that you share your success generously with the world. It would be consistent with many philosophies to pay 10% of your income to a respectable non-profit organization. This not only would be considered a tax deduction, but it can genuinely support and make the world a better place. Considerations for organizations can be your local church or congregation that could use the added funds for local needs, all the way up to a larger organization. Find something that you feel comfortable giving to, and somewhere that you know the funds will be handled responsibility. I would also recommend that you consider giving to an organization locally that you know can make a significant impact on the people in your immediate society.

Now with this idea, please note that it is irrelevant how much you are actually giving, but that it is 10%. If 10% is only $10 for the month, than $10 is what you give. If $10,000 a month is 10% of what you have earned, than $10,000 a month is what you give. As you start your business, you will find that you will start small, but that number will begin to grow. Never forget that $10 can make quite an impact at a food bank, and that you can change lives with the smallest of donations made on a regular basis.

This isn't all about giving, and is not entirely an altruist notion. You get something in return that is a greater value than what you were giving. You are getting the ability to magnify yourself. This is for a number of reasons.

Consider for a moment, as it was discussed, the notion of looking past the result and more towards the goals. Money is a result, not the action or the goal. Giving can be a reaffirmation towards that reality. To give is to recognize that money is not the core of your motivation. It is not ultimately what you seek after; it is only a consequence of what you seek after. You respect your money, and you respect the conditions or the society that gave you that money. Money comes from somewhere and from someone – it doesn't just appear. But by giving a portion of it back to society, you are creating an applied reality within yourself that money is something you understand, and that you respect the society that gave it to you.

For those of you who feel a force in the universe that governs goods things and inspires the world towards a positive end (whatever that force may be for you), this principle is powerful: When you seek to do good for the world you, in turn, improve the world with the ratio of your own improvement. It would not be a far step within your philosophy to believe that if that governing force wanted more good done in your hands, and was confident that you would be consistent in that giving, you could be given more so that more good could be done.

There have been many individuals with whom I have worked directly and spoken with on this topic who have expressed some unique realities. In sum, they have nearly all said that when tempted to stop committed payments to their organizations, they noticed their earnings decrease. Only when they resumed their commitments to give did they being to grow again. There are many explanations for this reality, but regardless of the explanation, the formula for those individuals were the same – give 10%, work hard, and watch it increase.

As mentioned before, don't wait to make this commitment when you believe you make enough to justify giving. Giving is not about the amount, it is about the character it creates in the leader. You can be a leader by giving $1 if that is 10% of what you made in your check. Give it, share it, and make that commitment. If you don't do it, when the money is so little, why would you trust yourself to give it when the money becomes larger. Why would you think that you would even actually get rewarded with such success?

RYAN DALEY

# Pay Your Most Important Employee – 10%

The most important employee you pay is yourself. You must make sure you pay yourself. Create an account which is moderately inaccessible. This would be something that you would require some effort in withdrawing from. Place 10% of every dollar you earn in this account. This is where you pay yourself.

This money is not to be spent; only in times of emergency, retirement, or secured investment. This is where, over the years of your steady increase, you begin to build a small personal safety net that can be surprisingly large over the years. Remember, it is not always about how much you make, it is about how much you keep. Too many people do not have any form of real savings.

You will be surprised just how easily $100 can turn into $1,000, and then to $10,000. For many of us, this small account will never contain the millions we one day hope to create, but it will create for us and our families a safe haven in case of an emergency as we work diligently towards those large checks. This also helps us in times of crisis not to be totally reliant upon our business. There will be tragedies in our lives and crises which will appear. If we are not prepared for them, and we find ourselves adding to those worries the need to work and increase a check for those periods of time, then we have not developed freedom at all. This fund can be used to support those dark times in our lives, and allow us in those moments the freedom to focus on those things that are most important – rather than on business.

RYAN DALEY

# Pay Your Most Important Supporters – 10%

Take 10% from each check and do something towards increasing the standard of living for your family. Buy them something that they have always wanted. Put the money in a fund towards a family vacation. Buy that video game that your children have been begging for over the last three months; or even the less popular, school tuition. This is not intended to spoil your family, but to reward them for their support in what you are doing.

This will also get them more excited about your own business choices. They can increase their support, as they see that there are overall benefits for the family. This is where you and your family can have a budget to enjoy the fruits of your labors. Let them be excited about the rewards of what you do, and you will find their support for your business increase. This will help as you find yourself out doing meetings late a few times a week; as they begin to see that you are doing what you do for them.

# Reinvest In Your Business – 10%

Particularly at the very beginning of your business, you will find that you need to reinvest in your business to help it grow. I recommend that this is done throughout all stages of leadership development and organizational growth. As your check increases, so does the amount that you have to spend, but then, so do your expenses.

The types of business reinvestment will also change. At the beginning of your business your reinvestment may look like increasing personal inventory, attending corporate events, and maybe even some travel. As your organization matures you may find yourself spending more on travel, on advertising and marketing, and even on team activities. Be open to what a "reinvestment" might look like to mature as your responsibilities to your team mature.

Place 10% in an account that is for reinvestment expenses. You may not spend all of this every month, but as it increases, when those bigger opportunities develop, you will find that you will already have the resources to put towards it guilt-free. You can move forward with your reinvestment, without feeling like you are taking away from your family, or taking away from something else important.

# Removing Your Nightmares and Fulfilling your Dreams – 30%

Everything else, the 30% remaining, should go towards your short term and long term goals. As your business starts and grows these goals will change as you develop as a leader. You will start with extremely important goals that can be fulfilled within a few months, and then will slowly start to move towards larger goals. It is highly encouraged that you start with the short term steps and fulfill them before you start on the larger goals, because there are some very important things that as a leader seeking financial freedom, you have to get a handle on first.

Your first short terms goals may be to pay off credit cards, student loans, or car payments. Do that first. Take 30% of your residual check, and place it towards the principal of your short term debt. Do this as many months as it takes to get out of short term debt – then work hard at staying out of it. If something comes up as a need in the future, rather than taking out more debt for it, save that 30% towards paying for it. As you work towards getting out of this short term debt, start with the smallest debt, and pay it off. After you do that, move on to the next debt with the next smallest principal, and put your 30% extra a month towards it (as well as what you would have spent in budget on the payment of the bill that is currently paid off). Go from bill to bill until you find your short term debt is removed.

From there you may start to consider your long term debt. Long term student loans may count here, but most people think about their house payment. Other goals may come to mind while considering your family goals and desires, as well as your family finances. Saving towards retirement or even that million dollar bank account might be an appropriate long term goal – either way, put this 30% towards removing your nightmares and fulfilling your dreams.

It is required as a leader to work towards the freedom of removing short term debt from off your back. This will add confidence to your business and your activities, and bring you a sense of freedom that everyone yearns for in this life, and that few people really find.

RYAN DALEY

# ABOUT THE AUTHOR

Ryan Daley is one of the most sought after individuals in the Network Marketing industry, both internally within the corporate environment, as well as for direct consultation with many of the largest leaders in the industry. With his varied education and experience he brings a comprehensive perspective to nearly every aspect of Network Marketing that takes on multiple layers of consideration and strategy.

With his undergraduate study in Behavioral Science and Psychology his focus quickly became behavior as it relates to an incentive based environment. He went on to receive his Masters of Business Administration at the University of Utah which contributes to his extensive understanding of modern business.

In a corporate environment he has done everything from generating start-up success through strategic implementation and marketing, to supporting the turn-around efforts of some of the largest companies in the industry. He has developed, launched, and adjusted more than fifty compensation plans successfully – all creating increased activity and behavior within their respective organizations. Ryan has been directly responsible for over 500 million dollars of increased revenue within his first decade of industry experience.

As a direct industry consultant with many of the largest leaders in the industry, Ryan has helped develop organizational training programs and duplication models. He has helped each leader increase their activity within their organization, and maximize their commission earnings.